GOD AND MAN

MASAHISA GOI

© Masahisa Goi 2002.

Original Japanese publication:
Kami to Ningen by Masahisa Goi
Byakko Press 1953

English Edition:
God and Man
Translated by Kiyoshi Emi and Mary McQuaid
Published in the USA and in Great Britain by
Byakko Press
812-1 Hitoana, Fujinomiya-shi
Shizuoka-ken, Japan 418-0102
http://www.ByakkoPress.ne.jp
All rights reserved.

First published in Japan in 2001 by
Byakko Press

Original cover design by Toshio Shindô,
adapted by David Lee Fish

ISBN 4-89214-147-x

GOD AND MAN
*Guideposts for Spiritual Peace
and Awakening*

Translated by Kiyoshi Emi
and Mary McQuaid

MASAHISA GOI

Masahisa Goi (1916-1980)

ABOUT THE AUTHOR

Born in Tokyo, Japan on November 22, 1916, Masahisa Goi was a poet, philosopher, writer and singer. Though he aimed at a career in music, he found himself spontaneously drawn to the realms of philosophy and spiritual guidance. At the age of thirty he attained oneness with his divine Self.

Mr. Goi authored more than 60 books and volumes of poetry, including *God and Man* (his first and most fundamental work), *The Spirit of Lao Tsu*, *Lectures on the Bible*, *How to Develop your Spirituality*, *The Way to the White Light*, *One who Connects Heaven and Earth* (his autobiography), and *The Future of Mankind*—to name a few. Of these, *God and Man, The Spirit of Lao Tsu,* and *The Future of Mankind* have been published in English. Translations of other works are now in progress.

Before departing from this world in 1980, he named Mrs. Masami Saionji, his adopted daughter, as his successor and leader of the world peace prayer movement that he initiated.

CONTENTS

Questions and Answers

PREFACE

My life blazed
With the desire
To serve as a thread
Joining Heaven with Earth.

Throughout my life, this was my heartfelt longing: to play even one role in bringing the ideals of heaven into fruition on earth, revealing the pure land of heaven and letting perfect peace and joyfulness be realized in this terrestrial world.

This desire was transformed into prayer and action as the flame of my life continued to burn.

While thinking only of God,
Even my joined hands
Vanished in prayer,
Leaving only the blue sky.

As I expressed through this song, my mind moved more deeply and quietly toward perfect trust in God.

Then,

Where the vibrations of Heaven and Earth
United, and became
The roaring of the sea,
The sun rose.

And so I reached a harmonious state of mind where I experienced heaven becoming one with earth and myself becoming one with God. I entered the reality of *Kuu*[1], and was reborn as one who could relinquish everything and attain all.

That was at a time when, here on earth, hidden karmic[2] causes had been triggered, erupting in the violence of World War II and leading to the defeat of Japan and the cold war, which seemed to be beckoning a third World War. This is how humanity had been—and still is—drifting gradually toward destruction.

What will become of the world? Are the days of the last judgement at hand as the Bible prophesies? Is the end approaching for the majority of mankind?

Faced with the karmic fires which push and rage in societies, nations, and the world, are our individual desires for harmony of no use? Are the world's ideologies for peace without meaning? Will heaven rescue humanity in the end?

Frightened by these uncertainties, the world is unable to embrace hope for tomorrow and everyone feels lost, not knowing where to turn.

At this crucial time, I believe that if humanity can understand its true identity and connect with God, it can rise above this uneasiness and confusion to reach true spiritual peace and awakening, and eventually bring about peace in the world. I wrote this book with the intention of explaining, in the most understandable way, about God, spirit, human beings, karma, and cause and effect.

I believe that even those who have no knowledge of me at all, as well as those who are already acquainted with me, will be able to understand the message in this book.

Masahisa Goi

March, 1953

Chapter 1

FOR THE FUTURE
OF HUMANITY

Since human beings first appeared on earth, how many times have the stars circled round in the heavens? How many times have the first frosts of winter settled on the land? In thinking of this, we can start to imagine how long mankind has been dreaming of, seeking, and earnestly desiring complete peace—a world without fighting or fear; a truly joyful world with no sorrow, no poverty, no disease and no separations.

From generation to generation, these desires have fostered the appearance of many saints such as Sakyamuni[3], Jesus Christ and Mohammed. They have allowed artists to leave their names with us, and have shown us a vast array of thinkers, politicians, scholars and inventors, working through vertical and horizontal planes and in every field imaginable. By now, it would seem that every flower of culture and civilization must have bloomed, and that every fountain of thought must surely have been exhausted.

Yet, even having reached such an age of culture and civilization, people in this present world are still far from complete peace, and are gasping under precarious living conditions with fighting, fear, sorrow, ageing and illness, poverty, hardship and separation. How can this be? In terms of outward appearances, clearly, the difference between modern and ancient times is like the gap between heaven and earth. The advancement of material culture has brought extreme conveniences to our modern-day life. If we looked only at these conveniences, it would seem that people today ought to feel happy, as if living in heaven. Yet what is the actual situation? Certainly, the progress in our living conditions has made it easier for us to get things done at the material level, and has given us some sense of comfort. Yet this sense of comfort cannot give us the power to resolve the anxieties of mankind. Though different in style, people today are fundamentally no different from people in non-civilized times, in that they are continually experiencing feelings of instability that could lead to collapse at any moment.

Why is it that today's lifestyle, with gas, electricity, running water, trains, cars and airplanes, where people can attain almost anything they wish for with the power of money, leaves them just as mentally insecure as they were in non-civilized times? It is because in the present age, as in ancient times, people's lifestyles do not rest on a firm foundation. People feel vulnerable, threatened by crisis situations that could bring destruction in a moment, even tomorrow. No matter how much the superficial standard of living might improve, unless we resolve such problems as warfare, natural disasters, the suffering of illness, the inequalities of life—and the most fundamental one, which is the fear of the death of the physical body—humanity will not find happiness.

Will it ever be possible to extinguish such miseries as warfare, natural disasters, the pain of illness and the agony of death? To this I reply *Yes, it is possible.* The great ones of old, Sakyamuni and Jesus Christ, overcame these hardships, and they taught and guided their disciples through their own experiences. Their disciples conveyed those teachings verbally and in writing, resulting in the Buddhist Sutras and the Bible. These have provided light and guidance to people's hearts up to the present time. Whether it be the Sutras or the Bible, both inscribe the principles for delivering humanity of its suffering and illusion. If all human beings were to perform such actions as are taught therein, it is certain that heaven would manifest itself on earth. Unfortunately, though, people have used those scriptures merely as mental and spiritual food without putting put them into practice. In other words, the majority of mankind could not understand the true intention of the two saints. Nonetheless, the influences they exerted have taken deep root in people's hearts, gradually turning into a powerful light that is about to reveal itself on the surface.

Now, the karma of humankind is about to disintegrate on a grand scale and the light of truth is about to shine brilliantly. 'Those who connect with truth will remain, and those who do not will go to ruin.' Before these words of a saint can come true, I shall describe in as much detail as possible the relationship between God and human beings, spirits, subconscious and physical elements, and life before birth and after death. I shall also write about how human beings can best live, and offer guidance on how they can discover a truly happy way of life.

Chapter 2

RELATIONSHIP BETWEEN
GOD AND HUMAN BEINGS

W hat is a human being?

In answer to this question, I would expect to find extremely few people who can clearly state what the human existence is. This question, which passes through people's minds without ever really capturing their attention, is the most fundamental one for creating happiness in the human world, and it is also the most difficult question to answer. When a person understands what sort of existence a human being is, and what exactly the 'self' is, that person has been liberated forever. When many people are able to answer the question, humankind will have been delivered of its suffering and heaven will be realized on earth.

Up to now, many philosophers and people of religion have confronted this issue. Those who were able to resolve it fully became awakened ones. Those who were

21

able to understand it partially became scholars. Others, who understood it incorrectly, terminated their own lives or else became materialistic thinkers or activists who served to further confuse the world. And since those who could understand the real nature of human beings have been few within each era, humanity has remained confused up to the present.

At this point, before proceeding to the main subject, I would like to briefly describe the views on human nature which, I believe, lead to human deliverance.

People who recognize that a human being is not merely a physical body, but that within the physical body there is something—known as *life*—which is actively working, and who live according to this understanding: these people have taken one step on the stairway to heaven.

People who have reached the thought that spirit is master in a human being while the physical body is subordinate: these people have climbed the same stairway two or three steps.

People who believe that human beings are created by God and are God's servants and nothing else, and who fear God's judgement in everything, but are cautious in their deeds and cling to God: these people are still far from a true understanding of human beings; however, if they do not hurt others, they are able to climb the stair-way to heaven.

People who think that human beings are creatures made by God, but that since God is love, if they positively keep acting in the spirit of love, unhappiness will never visit them: these people are also climbing the stair-way to heaven.

People who do not particularly think of God or spirit but just sincerely perform actions of love with a bright and straightforward attitude: they also are able to climb to heaven.

People who, though they know nothing aside from the physical world, can spontaneously perform actions of love with bright feelings, believe in the existence of God, and live with the conviction that this world will surely improve: these people are already living in heaven.

People who know that man is a being who accomplishes the creation of that which has shape in this phenomenal world by freely utilizing the divine law of life, with the realization that a human being is spirit, and that the physical body is one of a human being's embodiments and is not the true human being itself, and who put this understanding into practice: these people are awakened ones. Their minds are completely free from limitation. While having a physical body, they realize that they are, in truth, spirit. Knowing that spirit is divine life itself, they express their sense of oneness with God and others through their actions. Two examples of this would be holy people such as Gautama and Jesus Christ.

Knowing the true human being is the same as knowing God. No matter how hard one may seek God, if one's actions are lacking in love and sincerity, one does not know the reality of a human being and cannot find true peace of mind.

The preciousness of a human being does not depend on the greatness of the physical body, or on the excellence of one's knowledge. It is good to have a lot of knowledge, but if this knowledge is not rooted in the true nature of human beings, or spiritual wisdom (divine wisdom), it will, rather, entrap humankind into misfortune. Though the theories of the materialists are very elaborate, when they are put into action they create a restless society and disturb the world situation. This is because those theories are not based on divine wisdom. In other words, the materialists are not aware of what a human being really is.

As I did in the past, the majority of people in this world think that a human being is a physical body, and that the mind is a function existing within the physical body. They believe that a person lives in this society for some fifty or sixty years and then is reduced to ashes and disappears into nothingness. They are convinced that with death everything terminates.

Does the disintegration of the physical body mean the end of a human being? I promptly answer *No!*

Most people feel that a person is somehow born into this world by chance, maintains his or her physical body by eating and drinking, functions as a member of society, marries, raises children, then passes away and disappears into nothingness. The majority of people have lived according to this view, from birth to death and from lifetime to lifetime. Yet, not being wholly satisfied with this kind of life, do they not feel some vague and uneasy thoughts, whether large or small, recurring in their minds? This kind of life seems too meaningless and purposeless. People feel that there must be something else beyond this kind of life, but they do not know what it is. And yet, though they do not know what it is, they are not positively trying to discover what it is.

These are the feelings of the general masses. Among them, a few are unsatisfied with the way things are, and embark upon social reforms or join ideological movements. Others enter into the interior of their own minds in deep pursuit, and come to know God and spirit. Both are efforts that aim at breaking through the anguish that people are experiencing in their present lifestyle.

The masses are drifting. With the shifting of time, they are being carried right and left by the violent whirlpools of humanity's karma.

What good does it do to grasp at the whirlpools of momentary elation and anger? Though those whirlpools may appear to hold the highest of joys, they fleetingly pass away.

That which has shape is a shadow of that which does not have shape. If one sees nothing more than the visible, tangible aspect of something, one will not be able to rise above one's suffering. Even if social reforms are realized by changing only the shapes and forms of things, humanity will not be rescued from its anguish. Thoughts which adhere only to the world of material substances, or the world of forms or shapes, models, organizations and systems, are what ruin mankind—they certainly cannot save it.

Human beings are not of the physical body alone. God, the life that prevails throughout the universe, divided out its creative power into individual personalities; and those individual personalities are human beings, who strive to draw the perfect image of God within the world of shape by interrelating and cooperating with each other on the horizontal plane as they fully and freely command their given powers in all directions.

God is the principle of life and the principle of creation prevailing throughout the universe. Human beings are the children of God who are trying to activate God's life in the world of shapes and forms.

If you are able to understand this relationship between God and man, you will be able to live unperturbed by any fluctuations in this phenomenal world.

Now I would like to write about this relationship in as much detail as possible in the following chapters.

Chapter 3

REAL WORLD, SPIRITUAL WORLD, SUBCONSCIOUS AND PHYSICAL WORLDS

In the previous chapter, I have explained the nature of human beings in general and somewhat abstract terms. In this chapter, I would like to describe in further detail what a human being is.

Some theologians advocate the theory that human beings are karma-created beings, or the 'cause and effect' theory, saying that human beings can never escape from the world of cause and effect. However, I would like to clearly declare here that human beings are not originally karma-created. If they were karmic creations, they would have to reincarnate forever and continually experience lives of hardship mixed with pleasure—nay, lives of much hardship with little pleasure—and would never rise above them. If this were true, to be born as a human being in this world would be very unfortunate, and the existence of God would lose all value.

It does appear that the phenomenal world is surely being moved by the law of cause and effect. However, when we think of the deep and irresistible longing for God that flows in the depths of the human mind, we cannot help seeing the bright light within the true nature of human beings. I have deeply pursued the spirituality of human beings and have known through real experience the oneness of human beings with God: that they are children of God, and are even God Itself. Now I would like to describe the origin of human beings, which I have been able to realize through oneness with God.

A human being is originally light that comes forth from God. Light is Mind. God is all of everything: infinite wisdom, infinite love and infinite life. However, if God moves just as it is, nothing will appear in the world of forms and shapes. If infinity were to move just as it is, infinity would be forever infinity and would never become finite. However actively one [1] moves, it still remains one [1]. Unless infinity becomes a number of finites, or unless one divides itself into two and then four, the world of forms and shapes cannot be created.

At a certain time, God, who is light itself, suddenly radiated a great variety of individually distinct rays that had been previously kept unified. From that time forward, the creative activities of God began. First, God divided Itself into Heaven and Earth. Certain rays called the Sea Divinity, the Mountain Divinity and the Tree Divinity created the world of nature and set its life-activities into motion.

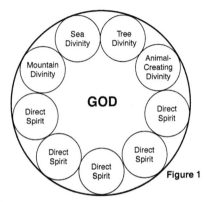

Figure 1

Other rays created the animal world. And the remaining rays, called 'Direct Spirits,'[4] created the human world. (Refer to Figure 1.)

Here God is One, and at the same time, many.

Now, this Direct Spirit, which is a ray of divine light, is the original 'human being', or 'man', that I have been writing about. At this stage, the first karmic cause has not yet appeared.

These Direct Spirits moved and radiated various waves of rays, creating the spiritual world and giving form to individual spirits[5]. Each individual spirit exerted creative power through the rays (mind) given by the Direct Spirit, and created the subconscious and physical worlds. At a certain time, they lived in the subconscious world, clothed only in the garment called the subconscious body. Then at a given time, they became engaged in the creative activity of the physical world, clothed in the garment called the physical body over the subconscious body. Metaphorically speaking, if the spiritual body is the interior, or the 'body', the subconscious (ethereal) body is the first layer of clothing, or the 'shirt', and the physical body is the 'jacket', or the heavier garment. These three embodiments are composed of vibrations of light.

As for the physical body, its light waves are very rough, its flowing speed is slow and its waves are heavy. The individual spirit is exquisitely fine light with a vibration that originally enabled it to move freely. However, while moving to and from the physical world, it unknowingly assimilated with the slow movement of the physical body, and gradually lost its fineness. Each of the individual spirits, who had initially created the physical world and who were engaged in the activity of forming the creation of God there, fell into the pupal stage, like the silk worm who weaves a cocoon and confines itself in it, and gradually its wave of light became impure. This is the same principle as the clearness of a rapid river and the impureness of a slow-moving stream.

The individual spirits then began to neglect directing their thoughts to the Direct Spirits, their parents, and started to engage in an easier creative activity by placing emphasis on waves of light (thoughts) that had accumulated in their subconscious and physical embodiments up until then. At that point, human beings began to restrict themselves, placing their attention mainly on life in the physical world. However, the thoughts, or vibrations of light, that were generated by the individual spirits when they started their creative activities were the original cause and effect (true good) that came from God. Thoughts that were conceived later, starting from the time when the individual spirits began to restrict themselves to the physical world, formed the first karmic causes. So began the tragedy of humankind.

In other words, to free themselves from limitation, each of the individual spirits, who had restricted themselves, tried to take freedom away from others. Instead of seeking from the Direct Spirits, who are vertically linked to them in parent-child relationships, they started to take from other individual spirits, who are horizontally linked to them as brothers and sisters. That is, they started to take from the horizontal rather than from the vertical plane. They began the history of struggle, using thoughts (knowledge) that had accumulated in their subconscious and physical consciousness, along with their physical strength, to fight against one another.

Occasionally, however, from the physical bodies in which they had confined themselves and are now still confined, they glimpsed through a gap the face of God and saw God's light. Then they cried out in prayer to the Direct Spirits for help, finding their former light among the accumulated thoughts. This was the beginning of the religious mind. The relationships mentioned above will be explained in illustrations. (Refer to Figure 2.)

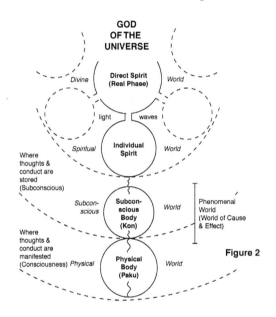

Figure 2

As shown in Figure 2, each individual spirit, while belonging to the spiritual world, created each subconscious body by using his or her mind (thoughts), and thus the subconscious world was made. This subconscious body became a place where each thought is recorded. In other words, it is the place where karma is accumulated. Memories, or records that have accumulated in the subconscious body, are caught in the brain of the physical body. They then become thoughts, which in turn become actions. This accumulated memory is called 'the subconscious,' and that which is caught in the brain is called 'consciousness.'

You may have had experiences of becoming angry even if you did not wish to, or of becoming unhappy even if you did not wish to. These feelings are caused by the stream of consciousness, coming from the subconscious body and subconscious world. This stream, or wave, always revolves, and the accumulated thoughts of misfortune attract misfortune, just as the accumulated thoughts of joy attract joy. Thus, it revolves like a wheel. This is called karmic cause and effect. I will explain this further in a later chapter. Now, I will go into a further discussion on individual spirits.

The initial creation of the subconscious and physical embodiments by the individual spirits is based on the same principle and is the same process of creation as God's creation of heaven and earth, mountains, oceans, trees and plants. The same principle and process also apply to the creation of animals by the Divinity in charge of creating animals. In other words, light waves were gradually materialized, from spirit to ethereal substance and then to matter, or from ether to elementary particles to atoms (electrons and electromagnetic waves).

One way to explain it is that the Direct Spirit gave its own light to each individual spirit and let each individual spirit create the physical human being in cooperation with the Mountain Divinity, the Ocean Divinity, the Tree Divinity, the Divinity in charge of animals and so forth. Therefore, the fact that a human being (in its divine, spiritual, and subconscious embodiments) is composed of light waves, and the fact that a physical body is composed of atoms, are based on the same principle as the laws of the world of nature, although the human creation is in a different category. What constitutes a big difference is that mountains, oceans, trees, plants and animals are created existences. They do not have consciousness of Self (intellectual wisdom). Within a human physical body, however, there exists the individual spirit, who is a creator and who unceasingly continues to self-create. This is very important, and the words of Shakuson, who said that a human being is a rare and miraculous treasure indeed, are true. Each of us ought to give serious thought to this truth—that animals are subordinate to God, while human beings are spirits divided out from God and are, from their origin, free and unrestricted beings—and we ought to feel a deep sense of gratitude for our existence as human beings.

The individual spirits pursued their activities in three worlds—spiritual, subconscious, and physical—manifesting themselves through spiritual substance in the spiritual world, ethereal substance in the subconscious world, and physical substance in the physical world. As time went on, the individual spirits gradually attuned themselves wholly to the physical vibration, and and came to behave as if they were merely physical beings. From this time onward, the sixth sense (intuition, deriving from outside the physical self) gradually declined, as did the higher intuition, or divine wisdom. The individual spirits became accustomed to fully relying only on the five senses. They began to think that what they could not perceive through their five senses did not exist. They began to think of themselves merely as physical bodies, and considered all the facets of their mentality and spirituality simply as functions of their physical organs. They ceased to perceive those activities as coming from their spiritual being.

However, it was recorded and remembered in the subconscious body that the individual spirit was originally one with other individual spirits in God, and the spirit sensed this beyond the conscious state. Accordingly, the feeling of affection toward others, or love, has not disappeared, even though spirits are clearly separate from one another in terms of their physical embodiments. In the narrow sense, this love prevails among parents and children, wives and husbands, brothers and sisters. In the wider sense, it prevails in society and humankind. Love alone is the road to God and light, and love is the only feeling and the only action through which human beings can find their original Selves.

In the material world, the world of forms and shapes, the individual spirits have tended to forget their own original embodiments of light (God). However, the idea that human beings are originally one and the same light wells up from the bottom of each human heart. This has been generating thoughts and actions of love in human beings, and has allowed the light to flow, however faintly.

The mind of God is called love, and the activity of karma is called 'attachment.' These two are what divide a human being's life into happiness or unhappiness.

Chapter 4

GUARDIAN SPIRITS
AND DIVINITIES

In the previous chapter, I have explained that human beings are originally divine. However, in reality the foremost problem is whether people can surmount karmic cycles, and what can be done to overcome those cycles.

Although karma[6] does not exist originally, a karmic cause, once it is formed, joins together with an indirect cause, or trigger, and produces a result. This result generates another cause, combines with another indirect cause, and produces another effect. Thus, karma seems to cycle endlessly, and this phenomenal world seems to end up as a karmic world. Since the individual spirit from God is now confined in the karma of the physical body, it certainly does not seem easy, or rather it seems almost impossible, to go beyond karma on the strength of each spirit alone. This is due to the law that a thought, once conceived and emitted, it is sure to return to its starting point. In other words, the transmitted thought, which is a karmic cause, returns and produces a result.

As time passed, the waves of karmic causes and effects accumulated and their layers became thicker and thicker, causing the physical ego of the individual spirit to be more and more inextricably entwined in them. The physical ego was generated by waves of rough vibrations, and it created a distinction between the 'self' and 'others' based on the material entity called the physical body. This brought about feelings of wanting to protect oneself above all else. Therefore, if something occurred that went against their own interests, people couldn't help struggling with one another to safeguard their interests. Moreover, the individual spirits were divided according to plus and minus functions[7], becoming man and woman; and as the physical population increased, the physical ego strived to protect only itself, its own family and kin. This caused people's karmic causes to deepen even further, reaching the state where human beings could no longer be awakened to their original divinity unless divine light were radiated through the spaces between their karmic causes.

At this time, the Direct Spirit of God, knowing this, radiated new light to free the individual spirits. This light is called Guardian Divinities[8]. Through this light of the

Guardian Divinities, those spirits who had initially created the subconscious and physical worlds were rescued from karma and took on the duty of protecting their descendants. They were called Guardian Spirits (also called Control Spirits). Among these Guardian Spirits, certain ones were assigned as Chief Guardian Spirits and others as Assistant Guardian Spirits.

The Guardian Divinities continually preside over many Guardian Spirits, and lend assistance to the Guardian Spirits. In time, each Chief Guardian Spirit gradually came to take exclusive charge of one human being, guiding his or her destiny. The Assistant Guardian Spirits came to take charge mainly of guiding the person in his or her work. When people receive intuition, or inspiration, it comes from these Guardian Spirits. This usually occurs in the midst of one's natural behavior. There are many cases where Guardian Spirits protect people through their own, unintentional actions, such as when you visit friends at their home without planning to, and something good comes of it. Or, just after you take a step to your left or right, a car misses you and you narrowly escape from an accident.

This system has been maintained up to the present. A human being is not merely a physical being as most people think, but comprises complex systems like the above.

Next I will discuss the life and death of the physical body.

What happens when a person dies? Where was I before I was born? From the previous explanations, I assume that you can more or less understand the answers to these two questions. But, since a more detailed explanation may make it easier for you to rise above karma and manifest your true identity, let me describe it to you.

In today's society, most people believe that when one dies it is the end of everything. They think that with the disintegration of the physical body, a person's life ends. There is nothing that conceals human divinity more than this thought.

When the physical body dies, it surely does not keep its original human shape, but turns to ashes. The form of the physical body disappears. Seen from the eyes of physical human beings, that person's figure vanishes forever. But will that person never appear in this physical world again?

When the physical body goes out of existence, it means that the cells of the body separate from one another. The physical body is a system composed of billions of cells through the mediation of many elements. In other words, light waves (thoughts), radiated by the individual spirit, constructed the physical body by combining material elements from the universe. Likewise, when light waves (thoughts) from the individual spirit stop working on these material elements, the structure called the physical body naturally disintegrates.

To put it in plainer terms, death is a condition where the individual spirit takes off his or her jacket, which is the physical body, and that jacket, having no wearer, is reduced to ashes since it is no longer required.

No one would say that if a jacket is torn, the wearer has disappeared. What has happened is that the individual spirit, who was the wearer or the 'contents', has moved to another world clothed in the 'shirt' which is the spirit's subconscious body. In other words, the true person has not perished, but has only left the physical world. I call the physical elements *haku*. The term 'haku' (also pronounced 'paku') refers to elements having a physical, or material composition.

The individual spirit who has left the physical body will live in the subconscious world for some time. A person's life in the subconscious world is almost the same as in the physical world, although the vibration of the subconscious world is finer than that of the physical. Because of this, in the subconscious world the things that you think appear immediately. It differs from the physical world, where what you think does not appear immediately. It may sound agreeable for your thoughts to appear immediately, but actually it is not. If your mind is not in good order or purified, you will undergo great hardships. This is because in the physical world, if you hate someone it cannot be known unless you show it on your face, and if you cheat someone it cannot be detected soon, and in some cases not at all during this lifetime. In the subconscious world, though, as you experience the emotions of joy, anger and sorrow, the results will occur instantly. Those who hate will be hated instantly in return. Those who cheat will be instantly cheated in return. All such thoughts as hatred, sorrow, fear and dishonesty immediately become the seeds and fruits of agony.

Through these experiences, one endeavors to purify disharmonious thoughts and habits carried over from one's physical lifetime, which have been recorded in the subconscious body. Thanks to these experiences, one will later be reborn in the physical world with a higher personality and better circumstances than before. This time a better life will be led in the physical world. In this way, after many rebirths disharmonious thoughts and habits will be corrected and in due course a person will become one with the Direct Spirit of God. The individual spirits in the subconscious world are called *reikon*. (*Rei* refers to spiritual elements, while *kon* refers to ethereal elements).

While in the physical world, the individual spirits are called *konpaku*[9]. In other words, spirit is divine, while *konpaku* is karmic—a temporary manifestation that appears while it has a particular function to fulfill. Thus, although the spirit is divine life itself, and originally lives in the spiritual world, once it has descended to the karmic world we describe it as *konpaku*.

Since human beings, in their essential nature, are spirit (God), they are intrinsically perfect, integral, and eternal. However, karmic activity, produced by thought waves from the individual spirit, set karmic causes and effects into motion. Through these causes and effects, karma cycles back and forth between the subconscious and physical worlds. In other words, through sequences of cause and effect, karma is born, then dies, then is reborn and dies again, and so on.

To say it in terms of Buddhism, human beings are essentially 'Buddha', which means that whatever maze of karmic cause and effect a human being might be in, the contents, or inner being, are entirely the life of the divine Self. My way of saying it is that a human being is the light of the individual spirit, and is the Light of the spirit emanating directly from God[10], and is the light (life) of the Universal God Itself.

Although many people have debated whether human

nature is good or evil, there is neither good nor evil in the original nature of a human being. A human being simply tries to put the creativity of infinite light (God) into action and to manifest the shape of God objectively. Good or evil are the interweaving and crossing of light and shadow that occur until God manifests Itself throughout the phenomenal world (subconscious and physical worlds). The shapes and actions that appear to be evil (shadow) are momentary phenomena that appear just when a greater good (light) is about to manifest itself. Even the shapes and actions that appear to be good are momentary phenomena that occur while a greater, all-inclusive good, or light, is in the process of manifesting itself.

As we have seen in the previous chapter, while they were in the process of creating the subconscious and physical worlds, so as to manifest the creativity of the Universal God with myriad beams of light, the individual spirits gradually lost sight of their true nature amidst the karmic causes that they had generated with their thought waves. At a glance this seems to be a mistake on the part of God, who has infinite wisdom. Since many people may have doubts on this point, I would like to explain it briefly.

This stands on the same principle as the previous

MASAHISA GOI

explanation of light and shadow. In other words, good is not simply good; evil is not simply bad. At one time during the creative process, individual spirits appear to be tossed about in the karmic causes and effects of the physical body and to have lost sight of their true nature. This is only the process whereby the individual spirits try to project the creation of the Universal God into the phenomenal world (subconscious and physical worlds), as directed to by the Direct Spirit from God.

However, from the beginning it was the plan of the Direct Spirit to rescue the individual spirits, who were agonizing in the above process, and to purify the physical world and let it manifest the will of the Universal God. Therefore, each Direct Spirit divided out its light, creating Guardian Divinities for the individual spirits. These Guardian Divinities freed from the waves of karmic causes and effects those spirits who had been engaged in the creation of the physical world at the beginning. These freed individual spirits became Guardian Spirits, and came to take charge of protecting, under the guidance of the Guardian Divinities, the junior individual spirits, their descendants, who continued to work in the physical world. The earlier, more experienced spirits became Guardian Spirits in turn, and finally more than one Guardian Spirit came to be assigned to each person. This still continues today. (Refer to Figure 3.)

Since primitive times, the history of struggle after struggle and agony after agony has kept repeating itself. Even at present, a hellish age, marked by the fear of war and the sufferings of ageing, disease, poverty, and other agonies, still seems to continue. However, the fact that there have been many saints and great people during these times who have contributed to humanity means that human beings, who are individual spirits from God, have sensed the work of the Guardian Divinities and Spirits, and have worked extensively in cooperation with them. This power has greatly accelerated the development of spiritual culture and material civilization. As the communication between Guardian Divinities, Guardian Spirits and individual spirits increases, this world will proceed toward true development.

At present, however, we are still in the process. In

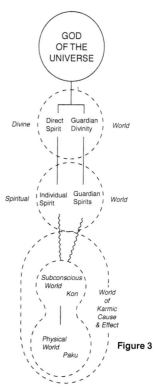

Figure 3

the future, after passing through this stage, the world of physical human beings is sure to become a perfectly harmonized world of light, just as in the divine plan. So no matter how helplessly close to destruction the present situation may appear, you need not be at all pessimistic or desperate. If only each person earnestly keeps accomplishing his or her own role, the day will surely come when you and the world will rise above this situation. I am absolutely certain that the day is close.

Chapter 5

HOW TO OVERCOME KARMA

Next I would like to explain how people can free themselves as quickly as possible from the waves of karmic cause and effect.

I believe that the truth seekers of olden times who practiced many types of severe disciplines to free themselves from their attachments certainly had great will power. But I would not think of asking modern-day people to do what those seekers did. In their present circumstances and way of life, most people find it very difficult to go to the mountains, to sit under waterfalls, or to fast, and the vast majority of people cannot carry out such practices.

These kinds of disciplines are given to the physical body to eliminate karmic causes such as materialistic greed, sexual passion, and various other kinds of attachments that grew out of the mistaken habit of viewing material substances (including the physical body) as true existences. But if the approach is wrong, practicing such disciplines has little effect. Therefore, I do not recommend that people attempt severe physical disciplines. I instead wish to elucidate a method that allows average people to free themselves from the above-mentioned kinds of attachments while living in their given circumstances—since this is the method that made me what I am today.

There are people who simply say 'If you wish to be awakened, first give up your desires!' or 'You are short-tempered, so get rid of that temper!' or 'Sever that attachment!' However, these people do not know how deeply-rooted human karma is, and so they cannot serve as guides for others.

There are also a great many people who interpret the law of thought (that a human being's world is the manifestation of his or her thoughts, and that it becomes just as the person thinks) as applying only to present thoughts in the physical world. They say such things as, 'It is because you do not show respect to that person that he treats you nastily. You must continuously and thoroughly revere him.'

They also say 'No matter what your husband says, you must obediently follow him to the end. Even if he strikes you or beats you, you must obey him faithfully. All your unpleasant circumstances are the shadows of your own mind.'

To a person suffering from illness they say 'The reason why you became ill is that you love rest and easy living. If you develop a hardworking attitude, you'll get well,' or 'The reason why you have a tumor is that you mutter and grumble,' or 'The reason why you suffer from neuralgia is that you entertain caustic thoughts,' and so forth.

Every thought takes shape in its own likeness. If one thinks of evil, evil will appear, and if one thinks of good, good will appear. This law of thought has been widely used among people practicing mental or spiritual cultivation only to condemn and judge others. I find this to be very regrettable indeed.

In the subconscious and spiritual worlds, thoughts manifest themselves immediately and return to oneself immediately. Thus, one can understand through actual experience which thought has returned and in what way. But even so, it is not at all easy to erase those karmic thoughts. Furthermore, it is very dangerous to try to guide a human being, whose body in the physical world is made up of very rough waves, simply by applying the law of thought in general, when one does not know what kinds of karmic causes the person has created, and, moreover, when one does not know what kinds of karma there are between that person and others. Far from being of service, that kind of 'guidance' will hinder the person's evolution and interfere with his or her purification.

To people who are offering guidance to others, I would like to give these thoughts[11] of Christ:

Do not judge others.
Love heals everything.
God is Love.

Nothing has more adverse effect than the guidance given by people of superficial love who have a penchant for intellectual knowledge and wish to be famous. I wish to strongly state that only people of deep love can guide people to happiness.

Karmic causalities are continuous waves that flow from lifetime to lifetime, from far, far back in time. They are not something that exists in the physical body during only one lifetime of fifty or sixty years or so. Furthermore, each individual's physical circumstances (disease, happiness, unhappiness) seldom arise as manifestations of thoughts conceived during the preceding two or three years. A person whom everyone regards as a fine, honorable person might be unfortunate, and a person who seems to be bad from any point of view might enjoy a good fortune that others envy. The examples of this are too numerous to mention. Thus, we cannot simply accuse and judge others.

Human beings have many different kinds of thought patterns, varying with the karmic causes of the individual. 'A''s good way of living cannot necessarily be imitated by 'B,' and the good things that 'B' can do easily cannot be done by 'A.' If a hundred people write a letter or a line, it will be written in a hundred different ways. If a thousand people write it, it will be written in a thousand different ways. But while some people have thought patterns that are vastly different from those of other people, there are also people whose thought patterns are very similar to each other's.

This is called analogy of thought. In other words, people's karmic causes are compatible or incompatible. For example, one person might wonder why another does not read a certain instructive book and might regard the other as inferior for not reading the book that has been recommended. But it is a mistake to look down on someone over something like that. It is also a mistake for a person who thinks that the music of Bach or Beethoven is truly wonderful to despise other people only because they are indifferent to it, and enjoy popular songs instead.

Among those who at present are devout followers of a given faith, there are some whose zeal derives from egoistic motives. On the other hand, there also are people who seem indifferent to spiritual questions now, but whose hearts are burning with pure love. One's true worth cannot be measured only by one's speech and behavior that are now being manifested in this world of forms and shapes.

In view of this, my method is to give each person the most appropriate guidance for him or her, based on the principles and laws that I will explain next.

In this present world, the thoughts, feelings and experiences contained in the subconscious and conscious mind are circulating in turn. What has been thought in the conscious mind is all recorded, just as it is, in the subconscious mind—the mind of the subconscious body. The recorded thoughts rise to the surface mind, or consciousness, as memory, and sometimes directly manifest themselves in one's speech and behavior. Then the manifested speech and behavior are recorded once again in the subconscious. This kind of circulating movement creates each person's future circumstances. It is important to first know this principle, and then to recognize the work of the Guardian Spirits who are making adjustments in the subconscious recordings that project each person's future. Otherwise, one cannot improve other people's lives.

It seems that, in general, a human being is thought of

as having only one mind. Actually, though, a human being has seven minds. To begin with, there is the mind of the great God of the Universe. Next, there is the mind of the Direct Spirit of God (God in the human world). Then there is the mind of the individual spirit. Next there is the mind of the subconscious body, and then the mind of the physical body. Additionally, there is the mind of the Guardian Divinity, who ranks at the same level as the 'Direct Spirit' of God. Finally, there is the mind of the Guardian Spirit who always accompanies each individual.

Being attuned to one's Guardian Spirits is the same as being attuned to God, and this attunement greatly promotes a person's progress. However, up to now the people who have known about this have been very few indeed. It is very difficult for a human being to progress only through psychological analysis or by applying the law of thought.

Furthermore, it requires considerable effort for a person to become truly attuned to God in this world, where most people live only by the physical ego, without thinking of God, to say nothing of psychological analysis or the law of thought.

Everyone works and makes efforts, wishing to be happy. Even so, not everyone is able to be happy. The secret to becoming happy is to become faithful—not to a physical human being, but to truth. In other words, it is to become faithful to God. However, since the term 'God' may seem somewhat far away and difficult to grasp, I advise people to become faithful to their Guardian Spirits.

In most cases, one's Guardian Spirits are the spirits of one's ancestors. Your own spiritual grandfathers and grandmothers are presently behind you, and with their spiritual eyes and ears they foresee what awaits you. They are always guiding you away from a dark path, toward a bright one.

This is just the same as when the parents of a small child hold its hand, leading the child this way or that. However, physical parents do not know their child's future, not even one minute from now. On the other hand, one's Guardian Spirits know very well what events will occur in their descendant's future, and they are always working to guide him or her toward greater and greater happiness.

The future circumstances of an individual are formed through the following process. First, each person's thoughts are recorded in his or her subconscious body. Then the various substances needed for projecting the recorded thoughts into the physical world are naturally arranged, tentatively constructing an initial pattern in the subconscious world. In due course of time, the pattern formed in the subconscious world will surface in one's actual physical environment, triggered by the person's thoughts in the physical world, which act as an indirect cause.

If there were no adjustment made by the Guardian Spirits, the mistakes in one's thoughts would become manifest, just as they are, in one's circumstances in the present world. If not for the work of the Guardian Spirits, each person's environment in this phenomenal world would become an exact replica of what the person had thought.

In other words, people who have pure thoughts would manifest pure surroundings. People who have unclean thoughts would manifest unclean surroundings. Those whose thoughts are filled with hatred would manifest a world filled with hatred. Those who have thoughts of stealing would manifest a world in which they steal and are stolen from. Those who have lonely thoughts would manifest lonely surroundings in their future. This is the law of karma.

However, the thoughts I have referred to here are not from one lifetime, lasting only fifty or sixty years in this physical world. They are thoughts that have accumulated through many lifetimes, perhaps three, five, ten, or more, covering a period of several hundred years, several thousand years, or tens of thousands of years. Those accumulated thoughts become manifest in this world, turning successively into indirect causes ('triggers'), then into effects, then again into new causes, which touch against other indirect causes, and produce other new effects.

There are people who think that their thoughts are only those conceived in the mind of their present physical body during the past forty or fifty years, and they say 'I have not thought such bad things, yet only bad things seem to happen to me!'

Other people say 'I am always thinking that I would like to get married, but I still have not been able to do so. So it is not true that there is a law of the mind, that things will turn out as one thinks'.

As long as one judges only from the thoughts conceived in the present physical world, one cannot readily nod in agreement. However, this law is an absolute law, the same as the laws of nature, like the laws of gravity or electric currents.

What one thinks will become manifest without fail. Simply by knowing this law, one can make more rapid progress than can someone who does not know it, and it will be easier to improve one's direction in life. However, if this law is wrongly applied, one may instead hurt oneself and others.

What one has thought will surely manifest itself. There are people who misunderstand these words, thinking that if they are fearful, what they fear is sure to take place, just as the law of thought states. Thus, their knowing the law has worked against them, and they continue to fear day and night, thinking that all that they fear will come to them.

One person was always worried about others and earnestly took care of them, and was poor all the time because of it. Another person lectured him about that, saying 'It is because you have a subconscious desire to be poor that you are always poor! Instead, envision yourself as rich! Because you have a desire to be poor, only poor people get together around you.'

After being lectured in this way, the charitable person began to have grave doubts about doing good things for others, and since then his charitable actions have been hindered.

As can be seen in these examples, if one thinks of or preaches only the law of thought (cause and effect), it is liable to bring about some really erroneous and adverse effects.

If one says or thinks such things as 'Because he (or I) had that kind of mentality, it has come to this!' and then forms fixed ideas about oneself and others and the harmful causes in people's minds whenever the situation looks bad, one's life will become quite barren of love and compassion.

To hurt oneself and others through a knowledge of the law of thought comes from ignorance of the true nature of God. God is Love. Because God is Love, God sent Guardian Divinities to us and appointed Guardian Spirits to guide and protect us. Because God is Love, God is working to purify and extinguish the disharmony that engulfs the human world.

Unless human beings trust in their Guardian Spirits, think of their Guardian Divinities and thank God, they will never be free from their karma, even if they know about cycles of cause and effect and the law of thought.

Guardian Spirits are always silently protecting human beings, regardless of whether people are aware of it or not.

Dreams are one striking result of this protection.

The question of why people dream continues to be the subject of a great variety of research by scholars across the world. Even so, the issue has not yet been clarified.

I say that dreams are the disappearing images of human beings' karmic causes.

Thoughts will surely manifest themselves. This is an

inflexible law. If, in accordance with this law, all thoughts were to manifest themselves in this physical world just as they are, this human existence would certainly have been destroyed a long time ago.

I say this for the following reasons. If the mind of physical human beings is thoroughly analyzed, it becomes clear that love turns into affection, which then leads to possessiveness or 'attachment'[12]. Grudges bring about more and more grudges; sorrow follows sorrow; a combative mind always feeds the flames of war. The karmic fires of sexual passion spread everywhere, and killing and wounding spread to all places, wherever one may look.

One of the great tasks of the Guardian Spirits is to skillfully depict a person's karmic thoughts and emotions in the form of dreams. This is done apart from the physical world, while the thoughts in the physical brain are dormant. The nature of thoughts is that once they become manifest, they disappear. So, if they manifest themselves as dreams, they will vanish. When thoughts manifest themselves in the physical world, the form of the thought may be caught again in the brain, and the same thought will be recorded once again in the subconscious body. (But even so, once a thought becomes manifest, it will disappear to some degree.) In the case of dreams, however, since the thoughts are skillfully caricatured and it is not clear what thoughts have manifested themselves, thoughts that come out in a dream will never be re-recorded in the subconscious body, no matter how hard one might try to recall one's dream with the physical brain after awakening.

Since those thoughts have been once cut off by way of the dream, one's karmic causality has disappeared by just that much.

Occasionally, there are dreams that one remembers clearly. However, because the images in these dreams have been depicted in such a way that the contents of the thoughts cannot be recognized, the significance of these dreams remains unclear. An exception to this would be a spiritual dream, shown by one's Guardian Spirits so that one can anticipate some impending circumstance.

Sigmund Freud, the psychoanalyst, interpreted all these dreams as expressions of sexual desire (libido), and analyzed the content of each dream according to the materials, scenery, names and so on, that appeared in it. This interpretation is entirely different from what I am saying, and I do not believe that it will be particularly helpful in freeing human beings from their sufferings and illusions.

It is not necessary to clarify dreams that are unclear. Rather, the thing to do is to simply thank your Guardian

Spirits for manifesting in dreams, and thus erasing, the unharmonious thoughts that would otherwise have taken shape in the physical world through an unpleasant future circumstance or turn of events.

I think that knowing this will turn out to be of great help to people.

Everyone ought to truly thank their Guardian Spirits for this wonderful work.

Guardian Spirits, who are able to work through three worlds (spiritual, subconscious, and physical) are modifying the effects of a person's unharmonious thoughts. In other words, they are improving the person's destiny (future life), which is now being formed in the subconscious world, or else which has already been formed and is due to manifest itself naturally in this physical world in the course of time. The Guardian Spirits are using all possible means to prevent the results (karma) of those unharmonious thoughts from manifesting themselves.

The people who know about or feel this work of the Guardian Spirits are very few, and most are totally unaware of the support that they are receiving from behind the scenes. Even so, the Guardian Spirits continue in earnestly exerting all their efforts to correct the future destinies of those people. This is what is known as the deeds of the Bodhisattvas[13].

Guardian Spirits correct a person's destiny in various ways. For example, a person who was scheduled to take a train that would overturn missed the train because he forgot something, thus escaping a life-threatening crisis.

In this case, thoughts from his Guardian Spirits worked on the person's physical brain, causing him to forget something by holding back the functioning of his brain for a moment.

There are also cases where Guardian Spirits make use of other people to rescue the person whom they are guarding.

For example, a person suddenly feels an urge to visit his friend 'A.' Although he has no particular business with 'A,' he goes to see him with the feeling that there is an urgent matter at hand. Then, the person finds that 'A''s entire family is about to commit suicide due to the failure of the family business. Dismayed by this, the person promptly helps his friend 'A.'

What happened was that 'A''s Guardian Spirits had sent thoughts to a friend of 'A''s who had a wavelength compatible with that of 'A,' attracting him to 'A''s house. 'A''s Guardian Spirits clearly knew that this friend would rescue 'A.'

Such things as in these two examples are always happening in the lives of human beings.

Guardian Spirits continue to protect the human being whom they guard at all times throughout the night and day, whether one is awake or sleeping, working or resting. They untiringly endeavor to purify the disharmonious thoughts that the person has accumulated. However, the way in which they rescue a person in this physical world is to let the person try his or her best, and acquire as much experience as possible. Then they rescue the person at the last moment.

Here, the point that we have to consider seriously is that the Guardian Spirits can most easily protect a person who always directs his or her thoughts to them.

There are no physical beings as easy for Guardian Spirits to protect as those who know the importance of their Guardian Spirits and who always thank them. For this, it is not necessary for people to know the names their Guardian Spirits had when they lived in this physical world.

On the other hand, when the Guardian Spirits earnestly send purifying thoughts to one's physical body, if one's thoughts are not even slightly attuned to one's Guardian Spirits, it is very difficult for them to protect the person.

In such a case, the best they can do is to erase, as dreams, the accumulated disharmonious thoughts (karmic causalities) as they arise from one occasion to the next. They do this by erasing those thoughts from the physical brain, after the person has entered the world of sleep.

To protect this kind of person, whenever they can the Guardian Spirits transmit thoughts to other people, and have those people provide warnings or assistance. When this happens, the other party has to have had a close relationship with the person in previous lifetimes. Or, the Guardian Spirits of both parties have to have had a close relationship in the past.

At times, though, the human being receiving protection is so deeply engulfed in karma that the light of the individual spirit is almost completely covered by illusions (darkness). Even though the Guardian Spirits put forth all their power to purify the illusions or take other actions, their light cannot penetrate the karma. When this occurs, they have no other choice but to ask the Guardian Divinity to rescue the person.

The Guardian Divinity then complies with the request and radiates a great divine light to the physical human being. This light pierces through the swirls of karma and reaches the individual spirit, increasing the power of the spirit's light. At this moment an interest in religion or spiritual matters somehow surges forth in the mind (brain) of this human being. This interest might be motivated only by a desire for personal gain, but that is all right. For this person, to have such a feeling is a step forward.

At this moment, the Guardian Spirits guide the person to a faith suitable to him or her without letting the opportunity go by.

In some cases, one might be transferred all at once to the subconscious world by the light of one's Guardian Divinity. In other words, one might suddenly die. This is done because this will be more favorable for the progress of that human being.

As can be seen from the above, Guardian Spirits become one with physical human beings and keep leading them toward the best path for them.

If human beings wish to improve their destiny and become happy, what they need to do is simply to entrust their destiny to their Guardian Spirits. One ought to always feel appreciative, thinking 'Thank you, Guardian Spirits. Thank you, Guardian Divinity. Thank you, God.' This state of mind is complete entrustment to God, and it is the best way for letting one's Guardian Spirits work to the fullest.

If one maintains this state of mind, it is quite certain that one's behavior will naturally become harmonious and well-ordered, and one's life will become easier and more enjoyable. The reason is that those feelings of gratitude directly connect the person with his or her Guardian Spirits and Guardian Divinity, and through this connection and the resultant light, one can break away from the karmic whirlpool of cause and effect before one is even aware of it. The original light of the individual spirit connects with the Direct Spirit, so that one truly feels and experiences the parent-child relationship that exists between human beings and God—even while one still has one's physical body.

When one does not know about one's Guardian Spirits and Guardian Divinity, and just aimlessly practices mental concentration or sits in religious meditation, creatures (thought bodies) in the subconscious world sometimes come to influence the physical body which has become, in some degree, 'empty' due to the mental concentration or meditation. In such a case, the person will come to have a peculiarly senseless atmosphere that gives an unpleasant feeling to others. This is quite unlike the sunny, joyful atmosphere of a person whose attitude toward life is naturally arranged by his or her Guardian Spirits. (This will be explained further in the next chapter.)

I do not advocate a method of emptying one's mind by sitting in meditation or silence. It is dangerous to try to empty one's mind when one does not have a good spiritual guide.

I believe that if one simply thanks one's Guardian Spirits and Divinity, and is receptive to their guidance, and is diligent in one's daily work, one will easily and naturally be connected to God, and can thus reach spiritual awakening.

Whatever kind of difficult situation may come before a person, it will definitely turn to a bright one for someone who is able to believe in the protection of his or her Guardian Spirits.

It is not necessary for you to investigate the identity of your Guardian Spirits, or to know what their names and family connections were during their lives in the physical world. The thing to do is simply to think, with an appreciative feeling, that one or more of your ancestors who is closely related to you, although you do not know who it is, is protecting you with a strong power connected to God.

If there should be some matter in which your judgement wavers, call upon your Guardian Spirits within your heart and ask for the right decision. If you do this, it is certain that they will answer you in one way or another. As I mentioned before, the answer might come from the mouth of another person whom you meet. Or, the answer might be known to you in a flash of intuition. In the case of the former, the first person you meet will give you the answer. In the case of the latter, your very first intuition will be the reply.

No matter how inconvenient that answer might seem to be for your present self, it is sure to be the way that will lead you to a better situation later on. You must believe this. You have to be very wary of the second 'intuitive' feeling, as it is the karmic reply. The karmic reply is always sugar-coated. Since many of these second answers seem very convenient, people are very often tempted by them. Because of this, it is important, at all times, to believe in your Guardian Spirits and to feel thankful for their protection.

The 'party of two pilgrims,' mentioned by the Great Teacher Kobo[14], means that a human being does not live alone in this life, but is always in a party of two, accompanied by his or her Guardian Spirit. This is to say that one always lives together with God. It is the same as in the teachings of Christ, who taught people that God is always with them. But most people feel that God is so great and so high up that it seems more familiar and easier for them to think of their Guardian Spirits, who have a direct connection with them as ancestors, and who at the same time are powerful spirits who are always protecting them from behind the scenes. This makes it easier for people to become one with God.

Also, instead of psychoanalyzing what kind of past mentality has taken shape in the form of disease or unhappiness, and reflecting on it, it would be better to simply believe that since all the adverse situations that have appeared are manifestations of karma accumulated in the past, and are vanishing into nothingness when they appear, when this difficulty is over you will definitely be placed in much better surroundings. At the same time, it is important to believe that since your Guardian Spirits are protecting you, the situation is without fail becoming better and better. Analysis of past cause and effect is likely to hurt a person, and it leads to a dark frame of mind, which tends to separate the person from God.

Since God is Light, God rejoices in a person who always has a sunny mind.

God is love. God is light. I am always living in the midst of God's love and light. Also, I am living under the protection of my Guardian Spirits. The past no longer exists. It is vanishing. Any kind of affliction is sure to disappear. To believe this, without digging up the mistakes of the past, and to keep one's mind turned only toward the light, is the most important thing you can do to free yourself and others from the whirlpools of karma.

It is important for us all to create a world of love and

forgiveness.

Love yourself and love others.

Forgive yourself and forgive others.

This is the best way to overcome karma.

Everyone, let us be compassionate with one another and let us encourage one another.

When your wisdom and power do not suffice, entrust everything to your Guardian Spirits. Your Guardian Spirits will surely take good care of things for you.

Chapter 6

TRUE RELIGIONS AND MISTAKEN RELIGIONS

The first question is 'what is religion?'

I interpret religion as being the way of explaining, teaching and clarifying the relationship between God (the Absolute Being) and man[15].

Following this principle, I shall consider the distinction between true religions and mistaken religions.

God is the source of human ideas, and is the origin of wisdom (creative power), love, and life. Consequently, God is perfect and integral, and is the symbol of wholeness and harmony.

Although they have within them this perfect and integral power, human beings, caught in the whirlpool of karma, have mistakenly taken that whirlpool to be themselves. Troubled with worries and agonies, that which tries to free itself from the whirlpool of karma is the image of a physical human being[16].

A person who has got out of the whirlpool of karma and let his or her inner divinity shine perfectly is called an awakened one. Sakyamuni was such a person, and so was Jesus Christ. There have also been other awakened people who manifested their perfect divinity.

To begin with, these people taught the relationship between God and human beings, revealing man's perfect and integral divinity. They put the truth into practice, and guided others to a state of spiritual peace and awakenment. If a person awakens to the reality of his or her perfect and integral divinity, it is certain that this human being has overcome karma and attained spiritual freedom.

The spiritual leaders who guide people to this state are apostles of God and are 'religious leaders' in the true sense.

However, what has been happening is that after these awakened ones have completed their lifetimes in this physical world, their various followers have started to hand down their teachings each in his or her own personal style. As a result, those varied teachings have spread throughout the world as individual religions, sects, churches and so on. In Japan, Buddhism flourished the most, and it divided into numerous sects. Gradually, religious proponents forgot the fundamentals of the teachings and, while carrying on vehement struggles against other sects, they went about busily trying to obtain followers. In addition to Buddhism, there were also Shintoism and Confucianism, and at present Christianity has become very active.

In this way, religions have taken a variety of organizational forms and have spread to each country in the world. However, it cannot be said that the religious spirit of humanity has deepened in proportion to the expansion of the organizations.

In ancient times, people used to understand spiritual truths through deeds rather than theory. They tried to know God by way of direct experience. However, from the middle ages to modern times, religion has gradually shifted from spiritual exercise to philosophy. Theoretical study has taken first place, and direct experience deriving from spiritual exercise has declined. Humankind has unknowingly drifted further and further from the original religious mind.

In time, religion came to be divided into three streams: in one were the theorists, in another were those who followed after the formalities of a sect or an independent religious group, and in another were those who truly sought to know, through direct experience, the relationship between God and human beings.

If it is only studied theoretically, religion simply

remains in the physical brain as knowledge, and the will of the great spiritual founders is not carried on. If one only follows after the formalities, the divine life withers and loses vitality.

God is all that has life, and man is also all that has life. That which lives forever and freely creates the world of shapes is God, and is man.

In a world that adheres to theory and is caught up in formalities, however hard one may seek, God is not found.

Religion is not philosophy. Religion is the world of spiritual exercise that goes beyond philosophy.

Religion is not a religious group, nor is it a church or cathedral, nor is it an organization. Religion is the spiritual practice and the teaching that makes human beings realize that they are life that is naturally connected to God.

If the essence of religion truly spreads throughout the world, and if humanity lives in the true religious spirit and in true religious faith, it is clear that this world will become a heaven filled with love.

Love is God Itself, and love is what works most powerfully to join human beings with God, to harmonize human beings with each other, and to bring human beings into harmony with all living things.

If, after entering a religion, the spirit of love does not well out in a person, he or she is not a religious person in the true sense. If, while praying to God, one does not enter the way to spiritual peace and awakening, one's view on God is mistaken and one's prayer is not a right one.

With respect to these points, one should distinguish between true religion and mistaken religion, and between true faith and mistaken faith.

Since ancient times, human beings have been seeking miracles and looking for new worlds. This mentality of waiting and wishing for something beyond human power, for events that are beyond ordinary human knowledge, is one part of the manifestation of the original divine nature and infinite freedom. In the depths of the mind of humanity, which always seeks a new world, there exists the realm of God.

This seeking mind became, on the one hand, the scientific mind which investigates, one by one, material substances that can be seen and touched, and it finally developed the modern theory that all matter is made up of waves, or vibrations. On the other hand, the seeking mind produced the awakened people who transcended the world of the five senses, entered the world of vibration, and further surpassed this and entered the world of the Origin that radiates all vibrations. These two methods have inevitably developed modern civilization and are aiming at the founding of an ideal world.

The awakened Sakyamuni, at the time when he surpassed his physical body and reached the original light, recognized his true existence as a body of light itself. From that time on, he freely exerted divine power and performed many miracles. Each of his disciples also demonstrated a particular kind of divine power, supported by power from their Guardian Divinities.

Many Buddhist theorists tend to place the greatness of Sakyamuni on his philosophical sermons and to interpret his miracles as mere tales to praise his greatness. However, it is because of those true miracles that Buddhism spread as we see it now. On this point, I clearly declare that the miracles of Christ are also true.

Religions without miracles do not spread far and do not hold strong appeal for human beings. On the other hand, many religions that only advertise miracles are vicious.

A religion of sermons only can easily turn into the skeleton of a religion. On the other hand, a religion of only miracles will make people all the more uneasy and disturbed.

Most of the established religions in recent times teach only formalities and lack appeal. Most of the newly formed religions preach of miraculous benefits in this world and do not release people from the source of their anxiety.

Even if one has received some benefits at a certain time or place, this alone does not prove that the religion being practiced is a right one. However, it is also too one-sided to say that in religious faith, worldly benefits are irrelevant and the only thing that matters is our happiness after death and in the future.

There are also people who say that it is wrong to seek benefits in this life through a religion, and that the only purpose of a religion is to let people see that the true existence of a human being is God Itself, and to reach their awakening, becoming aware that matter is empty, and that everything exists in *Kuu*[17]. This is truly a correct teaching, but when the attachments to the physical way of life are extremely deep, as they are in this world, if one only takes the view that the physical body is a temporary phase and not the ultimate reality, totally disregarding any interest in the life of this physical world, it will be just too far removed from the general population and I believe that it will bring true deliverance to only a scanty few people.

I think that for as long as people have a physical body, it is unreasonable to teach them not to think at all about life in the physical world. Therefore, it seems to me that rather than taking either of the preceding two approaches, it would be better to recognize the interests and benefits of life in the physical body and physical world, and also to recognize the existence of the subconscious body, and let people know about the subconscious world[18], and teach them how to live in the subconscious world after death, and then to let them realize the most important and essential point: that human beings are God Itself.

Here I would like to explain to you the world after death, which is, in other words, the subconscious world, and which I have not elaborated upon in chapter three. If at this point I do not explain the world after death, I think that you may find many points difficult to understand when I describe mistaken religions.

The basis of all the anxieties of the human world lies in the fear of death.

Whatever kind of agony one may face, it will not hurt the heart of a person who has overcome the fear of death.

There is no other event than death that so strongly arouses the concern of a human being.

Is death the end for a human being, or is it a transfer to another world? When this mystery is solved, it is certain that human progress will be accelerated.

A human being is not lost with the disappearance of the physical body, as I have emphasized in the last chapter.

Death is a transfer to the subconscious world. (Hereafter, when I use the term 'subconscious world,' it will encompass the spiritual world as well). The death of the physical body is a birth into the subconscious world.

The Japanese word *ôjô*, which literally means 'to go and to be born,' has been used for 'death' or 'to die'. This is because people in the old days were aware of the true meaning of death.

The death of the physical body refers to the condition where the individual spirit, who had been within the physical body and is connected to God, has shed the physical body while still clothed in the subconscious body. (From now on I will at times refer to the 'individual spirit' simply as 'spirit').

To repeat what I described in the last chapter, a human being is not a physical body, but is spirit itself. The physical body is the container of the spirit, and it moves according to the will of the spirit. Just as a car is driven by its driver, the physical body performs a variety of actions while being 'driven' by the spirit.

As I mentioned in the previous chapters, the individual spirit, who was divided out from the Direct Spirit, first created the subconscious body and wore it like an undergarment or shirt. Over it, he or she put on the jacket called the physical body. It is this 'jacket' which is habitually called a human being. Because they thought of the physical body in this way, the people who lived in the physical world were long convinced that the extinction of someone's physical body was the extinction of that human being.

To put it in terms of physics, the spiritual body is a body having a very high frequency, or a very short wavelength (a very fine wave), while the physical body has a low frequency or a long wavelength (a rough wave). The subconscious body has a frequency or wavelength just between the two. The individual spirit can have these three bodies—spiritual, subconscious and physical—as its own. However, to enter the physical body, the individual spirit must inevitably be clothed in the subconscious body. This is because when the individual spirit moves from the spiritual body to the physical body, there is too great a difference in wavelengths, or frequencies. Thus the need for a subconscious body.

The subconscious body has the role of connecting the spirit and the physical body. It also serves as the place where the thoughts of the spirit, and also the thoughts from the physical human brain, are recorded. (In this case the subconscious body is also called the 'thought body.')

With the death of the physical body, a human being (spirit) lives in the subconscious world, clothed in the subconscious body. In the subconscious world, as in this physical world, there are various ways of life and a variety of stages. One's life there takes shape in accordance with the thoughts accumulated in the subconscious body. If one's thoughts are filled with hatred, one will live surrounded by hatred. If one's thoughts are filled with deep love, one will live with people whose thoughts are filled with deep love.

Thus, according to the many different kinds of thoughts that have accumulated there, the subconscious world is divided into an unlimited number of stages. These can be roughly classified into three levels: the 'heavenly world,' the 'human world,' and the 'lower world.'

The highest among the three is the 'heavenly world,' which is the realm of people with deep love, or with few material desires, or few attachments, and so on. In other words, people who are close to the Mind of God live there. Also there are even more minute stages within this level.

As for the 'human world,' it is the sphere of those who lived average lives and earned average marks while they were in the physical world.

As for the 'lower world,' it is the world where people live who go against love, or have deeply rooted material desires, or tenacious attachments, or a fiercely strong physical ego, or are lazy, and so on. In other words, it is the world of those who are far from their divinity. They live there to have their karmic causes extinguished.

In the 'human' and 'lower' worlds, spirits can see one another's subconscious embodiments, and in this respect it is the same as in the physical world, where people see each other's physical embodiments. However, the speed of everything is faster than in the physical world, and whatever one thinks, whether good or bad, is immediately realized. Consequently, even though one may try hard to get out of the whirlpool of karma, it is extremely difficult to do because one's karmic causes circulate at a higher speed in the subconscious world than in the physical. (This is because the frequency of thought waves is higher in the subconscious world than in the physical.)

The way to get out of that karmic whirlpool is to once put a stop to those thoughts and enter a state of absolute oneness with God. This means to focus one's attention only on God, without taking notice of the karmic thoughts, no matter how hard they may revolve around oneself. How effectively the accumulated thoughts are purified will depend on how deeply one enters this spirit of oneness. The more one's thoughts are purified, the higher the sphere (world) in which one will live.

In other words, whatever hard, painful, or inconvenient things may happen to you, the thing to do is to view them as the now-disappearing manifestations of the karmic causalities that have surrounded you. At the same time, believing that now that they have manifested themselves, those karmic causalities are certain to vanish away, it is important to immerse yourself solely in oneness with God. The same practice is done in the physical world. However, unlike the physical world, where karmic causalities appear slowly, in the subconscious world they appear suddenly and violently, and you can hardly withstand the agony of it. When you think of this, you can see how much easier it is to have your karmic causes purified as much as possible while you live in the physical world, rather than having the same causes purified in the subconscious world.

You could think of it this way. If you borrowed ten thousand dollars (an analogy for karmic causes) in the physical world, you might be able to pay off the debt in monthly installments of five hundred dollars each. However in the subconscious world you would have to pay back the ten thousand dollars all at once, and if you did not, interest of another ten thousand dollars would accrue.

In the subconscious world ('human' and 'lower' worlds), practicing oneness with God is the best method for approaching spiritual awakening. Another way is to follow the guidance of your Guardian Divinity. As there is the aid of your Guardian Spirits and Divinity in the physical world, there is also the guidance of the Guardian Spirits and Divinities in the subconscious world (mainly the help from your Guardian Divinity). To faithfully follow this guidance is a good way to free yourself of your karmic causes. Since, in the subconscious world, there are also many cases where people are guided beyond their immediate interests, it is best to directly follow the guidance of your Guardian Divinity, even if it may seem to be against your advantage.

People who always thanked their Guardian Spirits and Guardian Divinity while in the physical world will also reap great benefits from it in the subconscious world.

Thus, after being purified to some extent in the subconscious world, a person may again be born in the physical world and experience a different way of life. After gaining more and more experiences in both worlds, he or she will gradually be led to a higher way of life. In the end, the person will reach the 'heavenly world'. After realizing his or her divinity, the person will live in the divine world or else become an awakened one who serves as a guide for others in the physical and subconscious worlds.

What it comes down to is that one's destiny[19] depends on how skillfully one purifies the unharmonious thoughts that have already been accumulated by oneself. One's destiny will become higher as the unharmonious thoughts are purified.

If a bucket becomes full of dirty water, one will surely pour it out and draw new water. However, human beings tend to want to hold in the dirty water (unharmonious thoughts) without letting it drain out. This is because when the dirty water (unharmonious thoughts) spills out, the place gets dirty. (This refers to the misfortunes and illnesses that occur in a person's life.) Yet if one kept on producing more and more dirty water (unharmonious thoughts, such as the fear of misfortune and illness, or grudges, anger, and so on), dirty water would always keep spilling from the bucket and the place would become unbearably dirty. To purify the dirty water, the first thing to do is to pour clean water (good thoughts, love and gratitude) into the bucket, and at the same time to keep mopping up the place.

To do this, human beings need to have endurance and courage.

Now, returning to the subject of the subconscious

world, I shall talk about creatures, or beings, in the subconscious world who exert a harmful influence on the physical world.

In the subconscious world there are human beings who, though they have already left the physical world, are convinced that they still live there. These people believe that the death of the physical body is the end of a human being. Their preoccupation with the physical body is extremely strong. Although they have physically died of an illness or injury, they think, in the manner in which we usually dream a dream, about the people who were around them when they were in the physical world (their immediate family and their descendants). They fix their attention on those people and follow closely behind their physical embodiments. Since they are convinced that they, themselves, still have their own physical bodies, though they actually do not, their subconscious bodies alone cover their thoughts and wander in the physical world.

If the soul in the subconscious world is someone who died of tuberculosis, he or she still holds thoughts of tuberculosis. Therefore, the person he or she is clinging to will gradually be influenced by the thought and can eventually develop tuberculosis. The closer the friendship or blood relationship between oneself and the deceased, the more liable one is to be influenced. The same applies to other illness and injuries.

In cases where the deceased tries to take revenge for some grievance carried over from before his or her death, the resented person is liable to receive some trouble.

In addition, there are souls who are abnormally interested in the physical world even though they have been transferred to the subconscious world. There are also 'emotional spirits,' or 'animal spirits,' that exist only in the subconscious world and do not have the ethics or morals that human beings have. Since these spirits and creatures are far from being awakened to truth, they are very much interested in petty affairs. Instead of inquiring into their own divinity, they have a strong inclination to make a great fuss by causing some incident to occur, or they may desire to be worshiped. Therefore, when they see physical human beings who plead with God to satisfy their selfish cravings, and who depend upon miracles (note: people living in a certain stratum of the subconscious world can see well the affairs of the physical world), these spirits and creatures mischievously transmit thoughts to persons having a certain kind of mediumistic constitution. (These mediumistic people are people who either have a large subconscious body, which is the undergarment of the physical body, or whose subconscious body is easy for spirits to go in and out of.) Or, they might borrow the physical body of the medium and talk through him or her, saying: 'I am the god of such-and-so.' Then they predict various occurrences in the physical world, which do come true in many cases.

There are a great many low-level and mistaken religions of this type.

In many instances, the founders of these religions are people with either an impressionable disposition or little scholastic knowledge. The reason for this is that intellectual-type people, even if very faithful, cannot help criticizing the words and attitudes of such spirits. This makes it difficult for the adhering spirits to freely utilize intellectual people's physical embodiments.

Low-level religious founders or leaders assume a very haughty attitude and speak in a vulgar way. Another thing they do is to predict things which it would upset people to know about. It would be all right to make predictions if the predicted event could be prevented by exactly following certain advice, but it cannot meet the divine intention to predict a future trouble from which a person absolutely cannot escape.

These 'spirits' are creatures in the subconscious world, and not Guardian Spirits or Divinities sent from God. These creatures pride themselves on surprising physical human beings just for the fun of it. They are like delinquent youths in the physical world.

One must not think that God is working through a person, or that a person is a god, simply judging from the person's 'miracles' of only making successful predictions or peeping into other people's minds. Even if a person's business has been improved by following the advice of the spirit (i.e., religious figure), this alone does not mean that the person has entered the road to spiritual awakening.

If one tries to cling to God only for worldly benefits one may risk losing sight of the road to one's divinity. If a religion fosters a base mentality of wishing to be saved by God without releasing the dirt that covers one's mind and without making the most of life, then it must be a mistaken religion.

And if a religion makes predictions that frighten people as a means of making them join the religion, then it is also a mistaken religion.

The original purpose of religion is to have people reach spiritual peace and awakening. If people's daily lives become uneasy or disturbed as a result of joining a religion, then the religion is doing harm to those human beings.

A true religion would have to be one that points out the way that lets people rise above their karmic causes and leads them directly to God, and it would guide and elevate them in that direction. A true faith would have to increasingly deepen and heighten the spirit of love and truth, and would inspire great courage for creating the full-scale harmony of humanity.

If a person becomes anxious or disturbed after entering a religion, either the religion is a wrong one or the person's faith is in error.

Even if one enters any true faith, one cannot immediately enter a state of spiritual peace and awakenment. However, the time needed for reaching such a state can be shortened to whatever degree, in proportion to the depth of one's faith and the seriousness with which one practices one's faith.

If you seek a true spiritual leader, the first thing to do is to turn all your attention to your Guardian Spirits and Divinity and earnestly ask for their help. Your Guardian Spirits and Divinity will surely send you to the spiritual leader who is most suitable for you.

When you meet the spiritual guide you have been longing for, you will have a feeling somewhat similar to peace of mind, or a delightful feeling, as if you have come home after a long journey or rediscovered something that is dear to you.

Suppose you are invited to a religion where the teachings are very noble and high, but after praying to your Guardian Spirits and Divinity you do not wish to go. Or, perhaps you do go, but after going you feel uneasy about it. In this situation it is not necessary for you to take part in the religion with a reluctant feeling. This is because that teaching does not suit your spiritual state at this time.

In everything, the first thing to do is to pray to your Guardian Spirits, who are the guides of your spirit and the guardians of your behavior. They will definitely cause a good leader or good partners to appear in front of you in this actual world.

I sometimes hear the admonitions given by people who are convinced that since God exists within each person, no one needs to receive teachings from anyone else. They give advice to their friends, saying, for example 'Since you have divinity within yourselves and are spontaneously being guided for the better, there is no need for you to be taught or purified by anyone else.' These sound like words of truth, but they are very much mistaken. The inner divinity always guides a person through human beings and through circumstances. Thus, there are many cases where one is led by the inner divinity to meet a certain guiding person.

It is really important for human beings to faithfully

practice the truth, and this spirit of faithfulness must always be based on earnest prayers that fully attune oneself to the guidance of the inner divinity (including one's Guardian Spirits).

One must not forget that one's inner divinity always includes one's Guardian Spirits and Divinities.

Even if a religious group itself is fine and right, there are many cases where the people who preach its teachings are in error, so it is also very important to pay attention to this point.

Also, even if a teaching is truly fine, and as far as the teaching itself is concerned, no one could teach anything higher, if the teaching cannot be put into practice, as is, in this physical world, it can be called 'unripe.'

To give an example, one might explain that a human being is originally without form or shape, is one with God, is light itself, and has a real existence that is free from all obstacles. One might then go on to say that it is therefore not at all necessary to mention that there is a subconscious world, or that spirits live after death, but that one should just intently and unceasingly think of God. This theory is true and there is nothing to be said against it. However, how many people are there who can reach a state of spiritual peace and awakening by intently and unceasingly thinking only of God? Are there any people who actually can, at all times, intently and unceasingly think only of God? These are the realistic questions. In an age like today's, when materialistic knowledge and information are flooding this world, it is almost impossible to guide modern-day people toward their awakening only with theoretical explanations about a human being's real and original existence, teaching people only that they have the nature of God and are essentially free from obstacles.

What spiritual leaders ought to do is to offer teachings about the original Self, the real existence and perfect reality of a human being; and while doing so, to explain karmic cause and effect and let people have a knowledge of the physical, subconscious, spiritual and divine worlds. They must explain that, though the essential Self exists in the original, divine world, human beings' karmic causes and effects travel about through various kinds of worlds; and they must teach and guide people on what they can do to actually confirm the existence of their essential Self and become an awakened being in the world of absolute reality.

In this regard, the work of psychic scholars and psychic researchers is also important, and mediums in the good sense are necessary, too. Traditional Buddhism, Taoism and Christianity are also helpful. However, if you become rigidly attached to one of them, not only will you be unable to reach your awakening, but also your phenomenal[20] living conditions and environment will not be able to reveal their essential goodness.

Therefore, what each person needs to do is try to know their own karma (including their personality and character), find their good points ('good karma') and develop them in real earnest. As for the 'bad karma' (shortcomings), after recognizing it one should let go of it without attaching oneself to it. The duty of spiritual leaders and guides is to recognize a person's strong and weak points and, based on this recognition, to guide the person in such a way that the strong points are expanded and the weak points eliminated. Again and again, the spiritual leader should nullify the person's weak points without calling attention to them.

Religions that explain karma but do not teach how to purify it cannot free people from their errors. This is because they cause people to get caught up in the idea of karma and to gradually lose the infinitely free spirit that human beings innately have. This drives people into a life of anxiety that is far from spiritual peace and awakening.

If one explains karma, without fail one must teach how to purify the karma, and one must be sure to teach that a human being's original Self is God.

The same applies to teaching cause and effect in terms of the law of thought (law of the mind). To point out that this misfortune or that illness is 'all the shadow of your own mind' is an example in point.

It is true that one's fate in the world of shapes and forms[21] is all the shadow of the mind. However there are not many instances where the illness or misfortune that a person is experiencing now manifests a mistaken thought which that person remembers. Most illnesses or misfortunes are manifestations of thoughts that were stored in the subconscious, including thoughts from previous existences which a person cannot remember. Also, there are many cases where a person is responding to the mistaken thoughts of ancestors or other deceased people who are in some way connected with him or her. I know very well that just telling people 'your misfortune (or illness) is the shadow of your mind,' without giving any thought to this principle, often hurts those people rather than helping them. Such words come from a lack of love, where knowledge is separate from wisdom. I do not think that a warmhearted, deeply loving person would be able to utter words that pierce into a painful spot or deep wound in another's heart. Rather, a loving person could not help feeling compassion for others in their misfortune.

However true the words may be, if the listener's state

of mind is far from those words of truth, the words will have little effect. Or, if one preaches a lofty ideal to someone who is panting of hunger, the effectiveness will be almost nil.

Eye of truth, come down.
Because you are so high
This world is dark.

So sang a poet[22]. But this might be the cry of physical human beings in general. A teaching that ignores this cry cannot deliver humanity from its errors.

'Cause one' must be erased by 'effect one', and 'cause two' must be erased by 'effect two'. 'Cause one' cannot be erased by 'effect ten', and might be deepened by it instead. (Note: 'one' stands for a low thought and 'ten' stands for a high ideal.)

Even if you believe that beef (words of truth) is nourishing, if you were served nothing but beef at every meal, it might be too much for you. And if, because you said that you wanted to eat dinosaur meat (wanted to know the truth), a whole dinosaur were placed in front of you, you would be able to do nothing with it.

Leaders must always be guided by love and divine wisdom; otherwise they will lead humanity into misery.

Now, since I believe I have set forth some general guidelines on how to distinguish true religions from mistaken ones, I shall go on in the next chapter to describe my method of prayer.

Chapter 7

MY METHOD OF PRAYER

Although I am continually busy each day responding to the people who come to consult with me on a variety of problems, fatigue rarely remains with me. At the moment when I sit facing a person who has deep karma, I feel their karma responding to my physical body as if I were receiving a radio wave. However, this feeling vanishes instantly and fatigue seldom stays with my physical body.

My physical brain is always void of all thoughts. I do not think things out with my physical brain. As the need arises, wisdom to fill the need is spontaneously conveyed from my divine body to the physical one.

Since I am not a medium, spirits do not move my physical body or speak through it. I look like the usual person, appearing in no way different from an ordinary, physical human being. I live and act within the framework of society's commonly accepted behavior. Fundamentally, however, my way of life is entirely different from that of a physically-oriented human being.

This is because I know through experience that my true, essential body is composed of light, and I clearly recognize that everything I say and do is governed directly by God (my original Self).

Ordinarily, there are always some sort of thoughts racing round the physical human brain. But in my physical brain there are no such thoughts at all.

This is because, at one time, I was compelled by my Guardian Divinity to undergo the training of completely extinguishing all my thoughts.

This was not the usual kind of meditation practiced in Zen or mental concentration. It was a continuous practice that went on for twenty-four hours a day without any break. (Details can be found in my autobiography, called *Ten to Chi wo Tsunagu Mono* in Japanese.[23]) If anything can be called difficult, nothing is more difficult than this. I had to train myself not to think of anything, to stop all thoughts. In other words, I trained myself to attain *Kuu*. Whether sleeping, waking, or walking about, all my hours were devoted to this practice. Over a period of about three months my personal ego was completely effaced, and I was transformed into my divine Self.

In the case of a medium, the medium entrusts his or her physical body to the will of the controlling spirit, and the medium's own self can sleep. But in my case, the objective of my training was for my ego to be perfectly extinguished through my own will, allowing me to attain perfect freedom of mind by going beyond the flow of karmic cause and effect.

Karma cycles endlessly from cause, to effect, to cause, to effect. To rise above this cycling movement, one must not grasp hold of the karma. Whatever kind of karma may emerge through an effect, its cause vanishes into nothingness when it appears. Therefore, when you send out only good thoughts, recognizing that unharmonious causes are vanishing and that things will become better as a result, a new, good cause is recorded in your destiny at that time. If you persistently continue this method, your subconscious will gradually be filled with good causes, which will properly interact with the good thoughts in your conscious mind. As a result, your destiny will take a favorable turn.

I have been teaching this method to people and asking them to practice it. Meanwhile, allowing no thoughts to enter my mind, I absorb their karmic causalities into my own divine life (mind). This meditation, or silencing of thoughts, is the state of *Kuu*, the true reality, which I was able to attain through the rigorous practice of stopping all thoughts.

The other party and I sit facing each other. In my true Mind I can see the light of the individual spirit in the other party. I also see the thought waves which that individual spirit has been continually emitting since past times, flowing in his or her subconscious body at various wavelengths. In other words, I see the waves of karma. I feel the person's karmic waves being absorbed into and gradually purified in my body of light. This is just like the function of a blotting paper. A blotting paper, however, cannot erase the ink that it has absorbed. But I can dispel the disharmony of the person's karma, that I have absorbed, as soon as I end the purification. The disharmony is dispelled by the light that comes to me from the original Source.

Those who have sat face to face with me unanimously say that they somehow feel lighter and refreshed. This is because their karma has been purified; and this purification leads them toward their awakening much faster than any words of preaching could do.

A human being's physical body is made up of cellular tissue, and each cell is composed of protons, neutrons and electrons. Further analysis leads to fine particles which are said to be particles of light. Scientists say that these particles of light are, at further depth, light vibrations. When human beings enter true oneness with their

Source, they understand that they, themselves, are infinitely expanding light.

In completely extinguishing all my thoughts, I freed myself from my physical ego. Consequently, although there exists a material body, known as my physical body, it is only an instrumental body that mediates light. When people sit face to face with me, the light of the original Source flows through my physical body into the karmic bodies (subconscious and physical) of those people. Then the karmic causalities that twine round those individual spirits are purified, and their embodiments become lighter and cleaner. So if they repeatedly sit face to face with me, they unknowingly approach closer and closer to a state of spiritual peace and awakening.

Either before, after, or during this meditation of silencing of thoughts, I frequently clap my hands to purify the karmic waves of the person facing me. I clap my hands at various rhythms, in tune with the person's karmic waves, since those waves are so varied. Through this action of clapping hands, light waves undulate along with the person's karmic waves and purify them.

In other words, through the rhythm of my hand clapping, the light waves of God wash away and purify the karmic waves of the person who sits before me.

In addition to this, I form a variety of signs, called *In*[24], with my hands, arms and fingers. This is for the purpose of guiding the other party to a state of oneness with their divine Self (God), and of attuning my wavelength of light with the other person's wavelength. To put it in plain language, it is the same as switching to different television channels.

In doing this purification, or prayer, I sit face to face with the other party and I also have the person sit with his or her back to me.

When the person is facing me, I purify the person's own karma from previous lifetimes. When the person's back is toward me, I purify unharmonious thoughts that are coming to the person from ancestors, relatives, or other people who are somehow connected with him or her.

I also give guidance, and pray that the person's destiny will change for the better.

Since I am not a fortune-teller, my objective is not to recount a person's past, or to foresee future events, or to critique the person's character.

My real wish and intention is to let all human beings know the existence of God and to let them know that they are not karmic existences but are children of light and of God.

I am working to awaken human beings from the illusion that they cannot find deliverance no matter what, and that there can be no relief from their suffering, worries and troubles. Therefore, I do not simply point out the negative aspects of a person's destiny, nor do I guide people with such statements as 'It is because your mind is at fault that you keep suffering from illness and misfortune.'

I respond to each person only with love, praying intently that his or her destiny will change for the better.

When I either hear a person's name or sit face to face with him or her, that person's character and destiny project themselves in my mind as if in a mirror. The reason for this is that my mind holds no thoughts of my own (since my own self exists in *Kuu*, or 'emptiness'). Thus, the other person's destiny, recorded in his or her subconscious, comes into my empty mind just as it is.

However, I do not tell the person all about those recorded conditions. I generally speak only about the encouraging parts, except in cases where a straightforward report will not hurt the person's heart but will have the effect of encouraging him or her instead. Thus I guide people in such a way that their habitual, mistaken attitudes and thought processes will gradually turn into shining ones. Of course, it goes without saying that I pray for each of them during this period with my method of prayer.

However fluently people might preach the way of truth, if they have but little love in their hearts, their presence sends forth but little light. A person of deep love, even if unable to preach at all, emits a brilliant light—simply by praying silently for the betterment of another's destiny.

Love is light, and light is God.

Acts of sincerity are the acts of God. Meditation of love is light itself. Words of truth, filled with love, are the words of God.

If you wish to improve another person's life, you yourself must first of all become light. To become light is to become love itself. You cannot become love itself if you entertain any selfish motives in assisting others, wishing, for example, to improve your own position, to exhibit your own power, or to be thanked. You must be motivated by pure love, really and truly wishing only for things to get better.

Pure love is the same as stopping all your thoughts (selflessness). This allows the light of the original Source to flow through you to the other party. The strength of the light differs according to the purity of the love. When the other person is ill or otherwise afflicted, any strain, such as thinking 'I'll cure him with my healing power,' will disturb the light and weaken it. In the same way, any feeling of uneasiness or anxiety will also disturb the light and weaken it.

There are people who undergo spiritual or psychic training because they wish to become healers or teachers with special psychic or clairvoyant abilities, but I am against this. The mentality of wishing to attain special powers is far from the Mind of God. I say this because God has already given each person his or her own mission to fulfill, and those who are meant to have authentic psychic abilities will be naturally guided in that direction by their Guardian Divinities. They will be given the necessary spiritual training, whether their present consciousness wills it or not.

As for me, I wanted to be a musician when I was younger, so I studied music. Yet before I was aware of it I found myself drawn into the path of philosophy, religion and spiritual studies. I was given many kinds of discipline and training by my Guardian Divinities, and in the end I turned out to be a guide on human life as I am today.

During that period I did not study more than did any of my friends, nor did I wish to have any special abilities. But it is certain that I always, always prayed to God.

The sense of that prayer was as follows:

God, please use my life for the sake of the world and humanity. Please let me carry out the mission given to me at the earliest possible moment.

This constant prayer never left my mind.

What wishes to have psychic abilities is the ego. The mentality that wishes for special powers is also the ego.

Such wishes or prayers of the ego easily trigger responses from low-level souls. Even if those prayers meet with their objective, and the person obtains psychic abilities, I think that the person's destiny will eventually come to an impasse unless he or she discards the ego. And I do not think that there will be anyone who is truly uplifted by the psychic powers of such a person.

A sincere prayer of love, an innocent brightness, an optimistic faith in one's own destiny: these are the qualities that connect a person with God. However hard one might pray, if there is malice in one's heart, or dark thoughts, or apprehensiveness, one cannot come in touch with God.

If you have a very anxious or gloomy frame of mind, the thing to do is to constantly practice looking up at the sky. Positive energy vibrations are always beaming down from heaven. Even on a rainy or a cloudy day, it is important to turn your heart and mind toward heaven. If you do, before you know it you will have a light and bright feeling. And I also suggest that you pray in the following way:

> *God, please fill my heart with love. Let me become one with my true 'Self', overflowing with profound love.*

Praying this kind of prayer every day, without fail, will lead you to a much higher state than if you visited shrines and temples to make a variety of detailed requests.

It does not matter what posture you take when you pray. Whether you are standing, sitting, walking, or lying down, the important thing is just to continuously and earnestly pray to become one with your true 'Self' that is filled with deep love.

To always, always hold a thought in your mind is much more effective than praying only at a fixed time. Therefore, if you continue to harbor thoughts of complaint, envy, inferiority, grudge, and anxiety over illness, through the functioning of those thoughts your life will turn out to be always dark and unhappy. Never forget that thoughts exert a great influence on your destiny.

Love heals everything.

What break through all misfortunes are actions that

originate from love.

My prayer is a prayer of love. I believe that wisdom is one aspect of love, and is included within love.

However, I would like to add that love is not emotional attachment.

Emotional attachment was born from love, and is inseparably related to love. This can be seen in the way the two words are combined in the Japanese word *aijo*, which means 'affection' or 'the attachment of love.' For this reason, even *love* is considered to be karmic in Buddhism, which teaches that 'love' is a source of illusion. The love of God, then, is called *Mercy* in Buddhism. What I have been writing about as 'love' is not emotional attachment, but is 'Charity' in English (Great Mercy, Benevolence, or Compassion).

However, I do not wish for people to make a clear-cut distinction between the two, thinking that love is good and that emotional attachment is bad. In this present world, love is inevitably accompanied by emotional attachment just as light is accompanied by shadow. Human beauty shines in a person who swallows tears while relinquishing an attachment that is hard to sever; and from this the radiance of love grows ever brighter.

On the other hand, if a person can easily sever emotional attachments out of coldheartedness, that is even worse than becoming easily embroiled in emotional attachment.

There is beauty in a deeply loving person taking care not to drown in emotional attachment. In the movements of such a person, I think, we can perceive the godly way of living in this phenomenal world.

My prayer is a prayer in which I become one with the other person and, enfolding the person in my heart, ascend to the divine world.

To pray is, first of all, to let one's mind be empty. It is to cast aside for a while the 'self' that has existed until now, letting only God live in one's heart.

One has to set aside all one's own hopes and wishes for a later time. If one lets only God live in oneself, all of the necessary hopes and wishes will be fulfilled.

The prayers of the small 'self' only make a person shrink smaller and smaller, and they do no good at all.

Instead, think only God. Practice only love.

Love, at times, can be extremely stern. But this sternness is entirely different from coldheartedness.

Love shows sternness to let the whole come fully alive, and at the same time to truly enliven everything and every occurrence. Coldheartedness kills everything for the profit of one's own self and one's own groups.

Each person must reflect on his or her own actions, to

see whether they came from the sternness of love or the harshness of a cruel heart. While doing this, one also has to observe what other people do as a reference. Then, one must fully utilize these reflections and observations as guideposts along one's path.

Coldheartedness disguised as the sternness of love, and emotional attachment mistaken for love: to overcome these two mistaken attitudes, human beings must pray to God and become one with God.

Believing that God has assigned me with the role of letting people thoroughly understand such deep human questions, I continue to pray each day, with many people, the prayer of *Kuu,* or true reality.

Chapter 8

CONCLUSION

Religious philosophers and specialists in religion may have different views on what I have described in the foregoing chapters. However, I have written this book not for academic purposes, but as guideposts for spiritual peace and awakening. After reading this book, if you can initially nod in agreement as to what a human being is and what God is, and if you can faithfully practice exactly as I have suggested, you will surely become happy. I have not explained any difficult spiritual practices at all, but have written about prayers and actions that can be put into practice here and now, on the spot.

What I would most like you to know, in reading this book, is that Guardian Spirits are always protecting each individual human being, without fail. When you pray, they will surely respond in some way to your prayer or guide you. If you faithfully follow the cautions and guidance from your Guardian Spirits, it is certain that you will successfully complete your path as a human being.

To believe this is the very first step toward truly knowing God, and this belief will be a great source of encouragement for you as you progress through your life.

Then, you will eventually reach the firm belief that you are with God, and that your spiritual guardians are accompanying you.

If you think of God only as being without form or figure, your thinking is still unfree. Indeed, God is originally the Principle of Life, having no form nor figure. However, divine functions may occasionally take shape as a particular divine personality and appear in front of us as a human being. So, if you firmly believe in the existence of Guardian Spirits and Divinities, and if you always thank them, the love of God assists you through various people and events at the appropriate time and place.

When spiritual faith fixes itself on one thing or one form, it turns into an attachment. There are people who, in an effort to reach enlightenment, hurt or torture their physical body and treat it as a hindrance. Yet I think that, in doing so, they are attaching themselves to the physical body. After all, our physical bodies were brought into existence because they were deemed necessary by our divine life. As long as we live in the physical world, we must treat the physical body with care and respect. We must each become a person who appreciates the enjoyments of physical life without damaging or hurting it, our minds always steady and unruffled. Otherwise, the significance of spiritual faith in the physical world becomes extremely faint. Religions and beliefs that disrespect the physical world cannot uplift this world.

It is my hope that, in the midst of your normal physical life, you will reach a state of true spiritual peace, resting firmly on the foundation of your life. To achieve this, I hope that you will maintain thoughts and actions of truth, goodness, and beauty while praying to your Guardian Spirits and Divinities without fail every day.

This, I believe, is the fastest way to enter a state of oneness with God.

As for people in leading positions and people who are working directly for their country or humanity, they are, of course, guided as individuals by their own Guardian Spirits and Divinities. Furthermore, the spirits in charge of guarding each country, and the Divinities who are watching over the correct development of humankind, are always guiding them too.

Leaders who are not attentive to this guidance—even though they were expressly given their high positions through their good thoughts and actions from previous existences—end up being carried adrift by their selfish intentions and desires, falling from their high positions, dragging others down with them, and leaving their nations and humanity gasping in the depths of anguish. This is why leaders, in particular, have to always pursue the Principle of Life, think of God, and pray. And when they pray it is absolutely vital for them to pray that their own country will exhibit its true nature and do fine work for the peace and prosperity of humanity. They must be aware that if they have thoughts of their own country taking the lion's share for itself, it is the same as wishing for the downfall of their own country.

Divine wisdom does not exist for the purpose of defeating the other party. Divine wisdom works through human beings to let them be enlivened and to make the most of themselves and others.

There are many countries and races in the world. This follows the same principle by which God branches into each Direct Spirit, and Direct Spirits branch into individual spirits. While maintaining its own individuality, each nation and race is meant to join in creating and materializing the divine intention in this terrestrial world, contributing its own unique wisdom and power in cooperation with the others.

Unfortunately, though, the world has not yet aligned itself with the divine will. Each country and race has been dispersing its respective wisdom and power, strenuously working to defend and solidify the nation that it constructed with its ego. When in doubt, they each arm themselves. When they arm themselves, they fight. When they fight, they are injured. Before their injuries can heal, they fight again. The losers are sad and the winners cannot rejoice in their victory. Such is the present state of this world.

As long as divided wisdom and divided power are manifested in disintegrated form in this human world, the result can only be relative victory or defeat, and the true divine world, the world of harmony, will not take shape at all.

From the viewpoint of God, how very sad it is that human beings and nations, without knowing the fundamental truth, are surveying each other and researching ways to suppress each other's strengths.

Each life is connected to the one, great life (God), and every kind of wisdom and power is derived from one Source. When the many varieties of wisdom and power are integrated, the divine world will immediately be realized on earth. It may be difficult to practice this, even if you understand it in your head, but an eternal, indestructible connection to God is definitely promised to the nation or people who first put this principle into practice.

Extraordinary courage is required for putting this principle into real practice. This is why each individual within a nation or ethnic group has to discover the true spirit of faith, and many great leaders must be born who know the true divine will.

I believe that the day will come in the not-so-distant future.

QUESTIONS AND ANSWERS

These questions and answers show the author's
replies to questions received before the
book's first publication in 1953.

Question 1
On the Birth of a Human Being

Q: Please explain how a human being is born.

A: After death, the life that a soul[25] leads in the subconscious world is determined by the person's past thoughts and actions. In that world, one experiences various sufferings and sorrows, or perhaps joys, and goes through activities that will serve for one's spiritual progress. Then, when the senior (high ranking) spirits who are in charge of one's spiritual education, or else one's Guardian Divinity, think that experiences in the physical world will be more beneficial for one's spiritual advancement than continued experiences in the subconscious world, the soul will be transferred to a transitional area to await rebirth into the physical world. There, the soul will wait until it is time to be reborn into the physical world. Except for very highly evolved spirits, the consciousness of the soul in the transitional area is kept asleep. If one were in a waking state, it would be painful, beyond the endurance of ordinary souls, to be transferred from the subtle vibration of the subconscious world to the rough vibration of the physical world.

However, among highly purified spirits there are some who endure the pains with an awakened consciousness and return to the spiritual world either after staying in their mother's body for a while or else immediately after being born as a baby. In doing so they become completely free from their karmic cause and effect.

Average souls are born without any memory of the time they spent in the subconscious world. Their past memories do not return throughout their entire lives until the death of their physical bodies. They go through the cycles of death to birth and birth to death many times, and thus they gradually get rid of karmic cause and effect.

The souls who are born have a close relationship with either their fathers or mothers in previous lifetimes.

Many of them have a blood relationship, and the frequencies of their thoughts resemble each other. This is why children resemble their parents in their physical appearance.

Occasionally, though, there are cases of non-blood relationships. But even in these cases, the thought frequencies of the souls to be born do resemble those of the parents.

Even though their thought frequencies are similar, there are some cases where a great person or else a person of small calibre is born vastly different from their parents. This is due to differences in the size of the light of the spirit, in the degree of the spirit's purity, or in the experiences accumulated through previous lifetimes.

In addition, the way a child is educated before birth (while in the mother's womb) also contributes to the difference between parents and child.

In the transitional area of the subconscious world, many souls are awaiting their birth into the physical world. Among them are several spirits who are related to a particular couple, say Mr. and Mrs. 'A'. It is important to know that the spirit conceived is the one who best matches with the thoughts of Mr. and Mrs. 'A' at the time of sexual intercourse. The vibrational frequencies of their thoughts and the kinds of thoughts they have at that time will determine the selection of the spirit to be conceived.

For example, if Mr. and Mrs. 'A' are engaged in sexual intercourse with high and pure sentiments, a high and pure spirit is conceived. If their thoughts are discordant, a rough spirit is conceived.

Therefore, the relationship between husband and wife is very important. If you wish to have a good and fine child, the mental attitude of you and your spouse at the time of sexual intercourse is much more important than either the prenatal training of the unborn child or the education the child receives after birth.

The baby's Guardian Divinity observes the relationships between the baby and each of the prospective parents through previous lifetimes, as well as the couple's thoughts at the time of sexual intercourse, and allows the baby to be conceived.

The period required for rebirth differs according to the karma of the spirits. In recent times, the period has been considerably shortened, and many spirits are reborn two to three years or else seven to eight years after death. However, it is not that the spirit itself is reborn, but rather that *Kon* (thoughts that have accumulated in the subconscious world, and are commonly referred to as 'spirit' or 'soul') gathers *Haku* (atoms that compose the physical body) and is reborn into the physical world. All the motive power comes from the origin of the spirit (called Direct Spirit), and the spirit's Guardian Divinity controls the birth. Therefore, while the person called Mr. 'A' lives in the physical world as a result of this rebirth process, the accumulated thoughts of the spirit called Mr. 'A', which continue from previous lifetimes, simultaneously carry on their own life in the subconscious world. This is like a double image. In other words, the thoughts are active through three worlds: spiritual, subconscious and physical. The power of the thought activity derives from the individual spirit, whose origin is in the Direct Spirit. However, this sort of explanation is so complex and intricate that you might find it satisfactory simply to sum up the whole process with the commonly used term 'rebirth of souls'.

I would also like to mention here that, in Japanese, this physical world is called *utsushi-yo* ('projected world'), which means 'the world that is projected from the spiritual world.'

Question 2
On Birth Control

Q: Please give us your thoughts on birth control, since it is being encouraged now and seems to be related to the rebirth of souls.

A: Until recently, almost all people involved in religion have taken a position of absolute objection to birth control, which has been treated as a major religious problem. Even though a portion of them are beginning to accept the practice, many people of faith are still against it, based on their belief that it disturbs the progress of spirits and runs counter to the divine intention.

As for me, unlike some spiritual leaders I am not especially worried about birth control, for the following reason. Given the present realistic conditions in this physical world, where most people still do not know the true will of God or the true identity of human beings, suppose there are couples with a small income to live on who already have seven or eight children and are afraid of conceiving additional children; or suppose there are couples who believe that they are likely to have children with inherited disorders. If couples like these are taught not to go against nature, or the divine will, because babies are granted by God and it disturbs the advancement of spirits to limit the birth of babies for their own convenience, it would only make them fearful and uncertain about what to do. This would have the effect of binding their freedom as human beings, and this goes against the real will of God.

Sexual intercourse between husband and wife is not only for the purpose of having babies; it is also for the exchange of love between them, and at the same time it is for the exchange of thoughts. It allows the strong and weak points of each to become well mingled, and it harmonizes the couple with each other and elevates them both. Giving birth to babies is one of the purposes, but not the only one.

If the only purpose of sexual intercourse were to have babies, human beings ought to have been created to have carnal desires at regular intervals, as most animals do.

I never think that practicing birth control before pregnancy is bad conduct. However, I earnestly hope that in practicing birth control, people will build a happier life for their families. My next desire, which is one step higher, is for people to enter the way that leads to their spiritual awakening, feeling confident that even without birth control they will have the number of children that is just right for them, and that the children will grow up well. This is what I sincerely wish for the people of this world.

Question 3
Whether our Whole Life is Determined before or after Birth

Q: *Please tell us whether our whole life is determined before birth, or if it can be changed after birth.*

A: A person's whole life is roughly determined by the cause and effect from his or her past lifetimes—in other words, what the person thought, said or did before being born in this world. However, it can be modified after birth if the person is faithful to his or her Guardian Spirits and Guardian Divinities, or if the person has a strong will to aim for what is good, or if the person's ancestors and parents have saved people spiritually.

What I always suggest that people do is to constantly thank their Guardian Spirits and Divinities and to pray. As most people cannot see their Guardian Spirits and Divinities, if they think it is nonsense, that is the end of it. But if they faithfully keep thanking their Guardian Spirits and Divinities, their gratitude will directly reach God and they will be guided so that their unharmonious fate, which was once determined by the unharmonious thoughts and actions committed in their previous lifetimes, will not touch against any corresponding trigger (indirect cause) and will not manifest itself. Or, even if it does manifest itself, the misfortune will be a minor one. This is how people's destinies are modified. (As for the good destiny resulting from their good thoughts and actions, since they can enjoy it as it is, nothing needs to be said about it.) This is how people who are faithful to truth are delivered from an unharmonious destiny.

In cases where people's will power is strong, there must be faithfulness to truth at the root of it. Otherwise, they will finish their life just according to their predetermined destiny, without being able to change it through will power alone.

If people do to the very best of their ability what is generally thought to be good and what they themselves also believe to be good, bringing to bear all their will power, their destiny will change.

In cases where their ancestors or parents have saved people spiritually, thoughts of gratitude from the saved people will naturally weaken the manifestation of the descendants' karma (as an unharmonious destiny). If the saved people are now living in the spiritual world, they directly assist the descendants from the spiritual world and guide them as Guardian Spirits do. This assistance becomes a power to modify the descendants' destiny, independently of the descendants' own efforts.

Even without knowing this principle, if you perform actions of love and truth, save people spiritually, and stop judging yourself, your destiny will change for the better.

Question 4
On the Difference between People
who will and will not be Reborn

Q: What is the difference between people who will be born again in this world and people who will not?

A: People who need not be reborn into the physical world have experienced the awareness that human beings are one with God, and that awareness is manifested through their actions. Since they are unified with their original, divine Self[26], it is not necessary for them to gain further experiences of overcoming karma (cause and effect) in the physical world. Thus they will not return to the physical world. On the other hand, an awakened spirit or Bodhisattva, who wishes to be born here to deliver those now living in the physical world from their suffering and illusion, is an exception to this.

As for those who have not yet reached the state of being free from the physical ego, but are considered by God as being able to gain the remaining necessary experiences in the spiritual world, and in that way to exit from the worlds of karma, they will not be reborn in the physical world.

The others will be reborn, and they will accumulate experiences that will enable them to know what a human being truly is.

Question 5
Is it Possible to be Reborn to a Different Sex?

Q: Is it possible for a man to be reborn as a woman and for a woman to be reborn as a man?

A: There are very many such cases. For example, if a person has thoroughly tasted the bitterness of a woman's life in her previous existence, and is firmly convinced that she would rather have been born as a man, her Guardian Divinity arranges for her to be reborn as a man, or vice versa. The Guardian Divinities may also arrange for people to be reborn to a different sex when that will make it easier for them to gain experiences that will help them free themselves from karma.

Most men who seem feminine, or most women who have masculine characters, have been reborn to a different sex from that of their previous lifetime.

In the spirit itself there is no distinction between man and woman. It is only in the worlds of *Kon*[27] and *Haku*[28] that there is a distinction between man and woman.

People often ask me if the God of Mercy[29] is a man or a woman. The God of Mercy, who is a personification of God, is the manifestation of man and woman combined, and represents the absolute existence of the plus and minus combination[30].

Question 6
Differences in Human Abilities

Q: I would like to know where the differences in human abilities come from.

A: Our abilities in this lifetime are all based on our experiences and study from previous lifetimes. For example, a person who studied mathematics well in past lifetimes excels in mathematics during this lifetime. Someone who had learned music well excels in music. All the people who are regarded as geniuses have mastered their art in previous lifetimes. For example, all such people as the child of six who is a genius at the piano, or the child of eight who can draw a picture at the level of a professional, and so on, have seriously studied their art in previous lifetimes.

When physiognomists or palm readers say that a certain job is well suited to a child, it is because the child's experiences from past lifetimes show up in the child's facial features or in the lines on the palm. I perceive this through spiritual insight, and guide people accordingly at intuitive levels.

Since experiences from past lifetimes are extremely important in this lifetime, people who are near death and continue their study and research up to the last hour are really living splendidly. Their efforts will be immensely helpful to them in their next lifetime.

We must not forget that success in any field cannot be achieved in a day, and that the efforts, studies, and experiences from past lifetimes form the basis of that success and play an important role in it. If we looked at this human world without thinking about previous lifetimes, it would seem that no world could be so unequal, imbalanced and unfair as this one. Thus it is no wonder that nihilists, momentary pleasure-seekers, and people involved in class struggles appear on the scene.

However, from the viewpoint of the divine will or of the law of karma, I have to say that those people are really unfortunate. Human beings should experience and study things that will heighten and deepen them, without neglecting an hour, a minute, or even a second. There is no other way than this for people to deliver themselves from their affliction. This is why I really feel pity for the youths who aimlessly shout 'isms' without knowing or even trying to know what a human being truly is, and let themselves get pulled down into the whirlpools of karma.

If you truly love and care about society, the country, and humanity, it is never too late to start devoting yourself wholly to learning what will heighten you and enable you to know, even dimly, what the true human being is, and after that to undertake activities. Life is eternal.

Question 7
Will Sutra Chanting
Really Console and Purify Spirits?

Q: Will chanting a sutra really console and purify spirits?

A: Reciting a sutra does console and purify spirits. Sutras are the words of Buddha, and they contain high light vibrations that lead people toward their spiritual awakening. However, the state of mind of the person chanting the sutra will heighten or diminish its effect.

Since the high light vibrations held within a sutra do, indeed, exist, those vibrations go beyond karma and reach the subconscious world. But if there is neither love nor faith in the mind of the people reciting the sutra, and they recite it only out of habit, or because circumstances have forced them to do it, their mental waves will not harmonize with the higher waves of the sutra, and its vibrations will not reach the departed souls in the subconscious world—which means that no effect will come from reciting the sutra.

If you recite a sutra, the most important thing is to focus your attention on the sutra. This allows your mind to become nearly empty. The light of the sutra will fill that emptiness and resonate to the departed souls who have some connection with you, resulting in the purification of their karmic causes.

If you ask a priest or a monk to recite a sutra, the manifestation of the sutra's divine function will differ according to the nobleness of the priest's character, the degree of the priest's spiritual awakening, and the depth of your love for the deceased person. The same is true for a Shinto reciting.

Question 8
What Should One Do
to Obtain the Infinite Supply?

Q: One religion teaches that God supplies infinitely. Does this refer only to heaven or paradise? If it is also possible to realize this in the phenomenal world, what can we do to obtain the infinite supply?

A: God truly is the Infinite Supply itself. To begin with, life is what first came from God, and life, itself, is what materializes the infinite supply of God. Therefore, people who truly strive to make the most of life will, as their life activity progresses, be constantly provided with the materials and other elements needed for making the most of life.

To make the most of life means to do everything sincerely, to the very best of our ability. There is no mentality farther away from God than trying to obtain the infinite supply while being lazy. To do our utmost in our present situation or environment is what complies with the divine will, and this is what links us to the infinite supply.

This means for each of us to smoothly accept our present situation. A person's present situation is a manifestation of his or her karmic causes and effects. To do our best in those circumstances is the greatest thing we can do to overcome those causes and effects. Furthermore, adopting this attitude is, itself, an action that constitutes our first step toward obtaining the infinite supply. What is meant by the 'infinite supply' is not that there is a pile of materials stocked in a house, but that the necessary wisdom, people, things, and situations come forth as the necessity arises.

Question 9
Is Possession by 'Animal Spirits' Possible?

Q: *Among Japanese people it is commonly said that a fox or badger sometimes possesses a person. I would like to know if this is true.*

A: Although they are called 'fox' or 'badger' this does not refer to the animal, but to spirit-like beings who inhabit the subconscious world. They are also called 'emotional spirits' or 'animal spirits.'

Among people who suffer from what is medically referred to as mental illness, and among some ascetics, there are many who are controlled or manipulated by this sort of 'emotional spirit.' Sometimes people who are constantly going to shrines and temples suddenly begin to make a variety of prophecies and predictions, and in most of these cases there is the influence of these 'emotional spirits.'

Although these 'emotional spirits' are commonly called 'spirits', they are actually *Kon* (karmic waves gathered together). In other words, they were born, or formed, in the waves of illusory thoughts, and are one way in which illusory thoughts manifest themselves. Their behavior is all based on curiosity or karmic emotion. They are not spirits who have love (God) inside themselves as human beings do. They are creatures who are entirely different from the true existence (true nature) of a human being. In other words, it is not a mistake to say that they consist of thoughts separate from love and intelligence, which are the most precious qualities of a human being.

Also, among human beings there are some who manifest neither love nor intelligence, and who, only for the sake of their own interests and emotions, become an enemy or an ally, and profusely praise or denounce others. Rather than describing such people as human beings, one has to say that, in terms of their thoughts, they are close to the so-called 'animal spirits.' When people with such thoughts go to the subconscious world, they become one with 'animal spirits,' and attach themselves to the embodiments of superstitious persons or ascetics who have low thoughts; and from there they mislead physical human beings[31] just for the fun of it.

The world of shapes and forms is entirely constructed by the projection of thoughts. Therefore, thoughts that in some way resemble the characteristics of a fox are perceived in the form of a fox by spiritual eyes, and thoughts that are in some way similar to the characteristics of a snake are perceived in the form of a snake. (Some psychic people and researchers use the term 'natural spirits' for these kinds of karmic conglomerations, but I simply call them 'emotional spirits.' This is because my explanation does not go into detail about the wide range of beings and spirits that are encompassed in the term 'natural spirits.')

The way to avoid being controlled by such 'emotional spirits' is, as I always emphasize above all else, is to be thankful to your Guardian Spirits and Guardian Divinity and to carry out actions of love and sincerity. I urge you to take strict precaution not to seek amusement from strange or mysterious things, or to harbor a desire for psychic powers.

As for people who think of themselves and are thought of by others as earnestly practicing their faith, yet have incessant misfortunes, there is a mistake somewhere in their way of practicing their faith. The same can be said about people whose faith disturbs the harmony of their home, or people whose way of practicing their faith and whose daily behavior are peculiar or eccentric. In many cases the homes of such people are affected by a 'possessing spirit.'

I think it is really dangerous to go from one temple, church or shrine to another out of curiosity, or to practice a faith for purposes of personal profit.

The first thing to do is to deeply reflect on your true Self and pray to your divine and spiritual protectors that you may encounter a good teacher who will guide you, not only in this present lifetime, but until you become truly one with God. Since your Guardian Spirits are perfectly united with you, if you always pray to and think of your Guardian Spirits and Divinity, they will definitely guide you out of the wrong course.

If you join a religion or spiritual group with this frame of mind, even if your initial motive for joining was for personal profit, in the end your path will certainly elevate you to true purification. And when you reach that condition, there is of course no need to be concerned about 'possessing spirits.'

Question 10
Why were Human Beings Divided into Various Countries and Races?

Q: *Since everything is One within God, why did God divide human beings into different nationalities and races?*

A: In the process of the self-manifestation of God, God has divided its divine life into a variety of countries and races, each of these having its own way of life. This is the same process as the one by which God created this world of humanity, expressing Itself through each Direct Spirit, and then through each individual spirit (refer to the main part of this book). Each nation, each human race, and each people has its own individuality and special characteristics. As each gives full play to its own special characteristics, they exchange their strengths and help each other. While still being many, the many are harmonized into one. In this way, human beings in this world are meant to manifest the will of God in the world of humanity. However, since it is very difficult for human beings to carry out this task by themselves, God is having Guardian Divinities and Spirits stay behind each nation and each race. These Guardian Divinities and Spirits are carrying on a great support movement from divine and spiritual worlds to realize the intention of God, which is, in other words, a return to oneness, or the creation of the great harmony of the world of humanity. It is a great, great mistake to think that world peace can be realized only through the peace efforts of physical human beings working on their own. If not for the huge scale assistance from divine and spiritual worlds, humanity would be gradually carried away by the waves of human karma. On the other hand, one must not forget that, in the world of humanity, human beings, with their physical bodies, have the key role, while divine and spiritual persons are constant supporters from behind .

The wisdom and power that come from the ego of the individual, the ego of the nation, and the ego of the ethnic group can never carve out the road to achieving the will of God. Unless all individuals, nations and races start again from a spirit of strong, deep, and exalted love for all individuals, all countries, and all races, neither a world nation nor world peace can possibly be hoped for.

The leaders of each country in the world must first realize that God, making use of many Divinities and Spirits, is now performing the great task of uniting all of the conduct of physical human beings into love alone.

It is certain that leaders who feel no inclination to just pray to God, with an open heart, will surely go to ruin someday. This is because under such leaders, world peace and the land of God will never be realized on this earthly world.

Question 11
On the Liking and Dislike of Religious
Services and Religious Matters

Q: Why are there people who naturally like religious services and religious matters, and others who naturally dislike them?

A: It depends entirely upon the person's karmic cause and effect from previous lifetimes. We cannot simply say that because someone likes to visit churches or shrines, he or she is a fine person, or that because someone is a member of a religious group, he or she is a pure person.

There are many people who have fine characters even though they do not visit churches or shrines, and are not members of religious groups. People who could be described as 'fine people' are those who are faithful to their conscience and have a deeply loving nature. Doing one's utmost for others with a feeling of sincere love is much closer to God than joining a religion or visiting a church or shrine only for motives of personal gain.

God is love and God is conscience. Therefore, it is useless for people to visit churches or shrines if they keep denying their conscience and have little love in their hearts. People of deep love who are faithful to their conscience and who, on top of that, belong to a religion in order to know God, are worthy of respect, and they will also find happiness.

Question 12
What is the Function of
the Subconscious Body?

Q: It is said that in addition to the physical body, a human being also has a subconscious body. What is the function of the subconscious body?

A: The subconscious body is a body that records a human being's thoughts and actions. It is a gaseous body that overlaps the physical body and has a shape like the physical body. The size and color of this gaseous body tell very well about the height of one's spirituality, and about one's character and destiny. When people say that they have seen a ghost, or soul, what they have seen is the subconscious body (including the thought body), not the spirit. The word *soul* is used to describe the condition where the individual spirit is enveloped in the subconscious body. In other words, it refers to the individual spirit, residing in the subconscious world.

The size and color of the subconscious body differ from one person to another. (Note: the accumulation of thoughts and deeds are what give the subconscious body its color). People with a large subconscious body are generally enthusiastic about religion, and some of them visit churches and shrines indiscriminately. A person who easily receives thought vibrations from other people and is affected by those vibrations, or who easily responds to thought waves from the subconscious world is, in most cases, a person with a large subconscious body. When the thoughts accumulated in the subconscious body are murky, or soiled, the person is liable to be controlled by lower level thought waves. A person whose subconscious body is pure can easily receive inspiration from high-level spirits.

The lighter the color of the subconscious body, the purer and cleaner the subconscious body is. When it brightens to a golden color, the subconscious body, as such, has already ceased to exist, and the golden color indicates that the light of God is shining brightly. The darker and heavier the color looks, the more soiled the subconscious body. If the color has shades of violet and blue, it indicates nobleness of character. When you meet a person and feel that he or she radiates a perfectly clear and pure atmosphere, it can usually be taken as a sure sign that the person has a noble character.

In any case, if you always orient yourself toward good thoughts and actions of love, you will eventually be able to carry out actions of love in a natural way without especially trying to. The physical life is not everything for a human being. Life in the subconscious and spiritual worlds awaits you behind this physical life, and you need to purify your thoughts and correct your actions while you live in the physical world. It is important for human beings to thoroughly reflect upon this truth.

Question 13
Difference between Christianity and
Buddhism in Recognition of the Creator

Q: It is generally thought that a Creator is recognized in Christianity but not in Buddhism. What are your thoughts on this?

A: This is by no means a simple question. In terms of Christianity, everything that has life was created by God. This is, of course, not a mistake. In Buddhism, it is explained, in the doctrine of the twelve causes and effects, that everything in this world was produced through lightlessness; and on the other hand it is also explained that behind this, everything has divinity—the nature of Buddha. I think that these two explanations, taken together, are really a marvellous way to describe the truth.

True Buddhism does not come alive solely from the doctrine of the twelve causes and effects and the teaching that everything was born from lightlessness. Likewise, the greatness of Sakyamuni does not arise solely from the teaching that divinity exists in everything.

Christianity, like Buddhism, teaches that God dwells

within, and it also teaches that one has to reap the seeds that one has sown—the same principle as cause and effect, taught in Buddhism.

However, the Christian explanation might be interpreted to mean that the God of the Universe, Itself, created the world of shapes and forms directly, whereas Buddhism explains that this world of human beings (including the subconscious world) was created through karma. The Christian explanation seems simpler and easier to understand, and it allows people to follow God more faithfully and subordinately. Moreover, in Christianity there is Jesus, who intermediates between God and human beings. Through Jesus, one's sin is pardoned by God and one is guided to heaven. This coincides with the teaching of the Shinshu sect of Buddhism in Japan that if one devotedly and wholeheartedly recites the sacred name of Amitabha, placing all one's trust in Amitabha, who exists in the western paradise, one will surely be reborn in paradise after one's death in this world.

The difference between the two is simply that the former refers to Jesus Christ while the latter refers to Amitabha.

In Christianity, human beings are thought of as creations of the Universal God. This has been taken to mean that even our physical embodiments were created directly by the Universal God. This way of thinking, taken alone, results in human beings becoming separate from and subordinate to God—unfree existences who are wholly controlled by a force outside themselves.

While, on the one hand, the Bible sets forth this concept of a Creator, on the other hand it also teaches of the God who exists within; and it frequently teaches that since God is love, a person who has done actions of love and has been faithful to truth (God) can enter the realm of God. In Buddhism, it is taught that one's karma constructs one's destiny, and that to overcome karma one needs to empty one's mind and awaken to the divinity that exists within. On this point, the teachings of Christianity and Buddhism do not differ except that they are presented in reverse order, as if the front of one were the back of the other, and vice versa.

One principal difference between Christianity and Buddhism is that in Buddhism, the Kegon[32] Sutra and others often depict the solemnity, beauty and splendor of the Real World and the world of the divine Self, and Buddhism describes various spiritual beings, and the spiritual world, using the word *God*. In this respect, Buddhism explains the divine Self (God) and the human world from more sides.

In Christianity, the understanding is that human beings were created by God, and their physical existence is that of a created object. Yet at the same time, God, the Creator, solemnly lives within the created physical human being. Therefore, unless they follow the voice of the inner God, human beings cannot rise above their suffering. The wisdom and power of the physical human being who forgets God will only produce more and more sin (karma), and that is why Jesus shouldered the sins of humanity and was crucified. Therefore, it is taught that people should entrust themselves to the mercy of Jesus Christ, forget the sins of the past, do works of love, and live with a faithful heart.

In summary, if you understand their contents well, the teaching of the Creator is the same as the teaching of karma, so each person may think about it in the way that suits him or her best. (As my thoughts are described in detail in the main text of this book, please read them together with the Bible or the Buddhist Sutras.)

Question 14
Why does Misfortune Continue Though You Live with Love and Appreciation?

Q: I've been doing my best to carry out actions of love and live each day with thankfulness. Yet illness and misfortune do not cease from one to the next. What on earth am I to do about it?

A: There are many people for whom unfortunate events do not easily disappear even though they continue to do good deeds, but it is nothing to be anxious about. This is a process through which the people themselves, or else their families and relatives, progress forward. In other words, the 'bad karma' accumulated through previous lifetimes, either by the person or by his or her ancestors, reveals itself clearly on the surface during the time allotted to that person. These manifestations are vanishing away, one after the other, as soon as they appear.

Since, in addition to the physical world, a human being also lives in subconscious and spiritual worlds, it is better for the happiness of that person, and his or her ancestors or descendants, to erase as much disharmonious karma from past lifetimes as possible while one lives in the physical world, where hardships are the lightest. This is why it sometimes happens that the more good deeds one does, the more misfortunes manifest themselves. But these are not real misfortunes. It is merely that misfortunes from the subconscious world have manifested themselves early.

If the misfortunes were kept latent for a longer period of time, they would emerge at some future time at a magnitude several times greater than what the person is suffering now.

Therefore, you must firmly believe that whatever misfortunes may manifest themselves, your disharmonious karma, and that of your ancestors, will completely vanish away through this manifestation.

There is absolutely no reason for God to ever give misfortunes to people who do good deeds. I clearly declare that this never happens. So, after reflecting in depth upon your thoughts and actions, if you can believe that there was nothing wrong in them, you should be positively convinced that your misfortunes are the disappearing manifestations of karma, and that from now on your life will definitely get better. This kind of courage, itself, is prayer. This is what uplifts and saves you and your surroundings.

You might be wondering whether people who do not encounter much misfortune in this lifetime will suffer in the subconscious world. This is not necessarily so. People who have accumulated good deeds in previous lifetimes do not run into much misfortune in this lifetime. Also, there are also people who do not seem to have much talent, yet are endowed with unexpected financial power and spend their whole lives happily, both in appearance and in actuality. Because these are the results of shining causes from previous lifetimes, there is no reason to assume that these people will suffer after they move to the subconscious world.

In addition to the karmic causes from previous lifetimes, a human being's thoughts and actions in this present world (the phenomenal world) determine the course of this life, and they also form a deep connection with the person's future destiny.

In any case, if you can sense that a human being is, in truth, spirit, and is a free, unrestricted being who is not mired in karma, and if you reach a state where you are never influenced by any karmic movements, phenomenal misfortunes will suddenly disappear and will never appear again. You will then be able to enter the divine world that surpasses karmic cycles of death and rebirth.

Question 15
What if a Religion Asks you to Abolish your Traditional Altars?

Q: A certain religion requires that, after joining it, you give up your Shinto and Buddhist household altars and all other related items, and hang up and revere only the mandala[33]. Is it good to do this sort of thing?

A: The essence of religion is to bring human beings back into oneness with the Divine Mind and to let them enter a state of spiritual peace and awakenment. Worldly benefits will naturally follow as accompanying phenomena. Before they choose a religion, it is necessary for people to know this essential point.

When a religion fixes itself on one pattern or model, it has already started to bind the free nature of truth. This is why I do not take the method of instructing people not to do this or that, or of setting up conditions only in terms of outward forms.

As I understand it, in the religion that you are asking about, the object of reverence, or everything, is believed to exist in the mandala, and all other things are deemed unnecessary. If you can affirm this, that is fine. If not, you should flatly refuse to join the religion. Just keep it in mind that the main point of religion is for your spiritual peace and awakening.

What must be known here is that spirits[34] live in the subconscious world after passing away from the physical world, and that a religious sect to which a spirit belonged when it left the physical body—or else the religious sect of the spirit's ancestor—forms a connection with the posthumous Buddhist name that is placed in the Buddhist household altar, and for this reason the memorial service offered by the people in this world through the posthumous name reaches the spirit more effectively. However, this is not relevant for people who can transcend this process in offering blessings for departed spirits. These are people who clearly know that since God exists within themselves, when they bring out the inner God through earnest prayer, the divinity of the departed spirits will also be brought out, and their prayer will serve as a great purification which will assist the departed spirits in progressing toward a higher world. Aside from those clear-minded people, though, I think it would be better for people of an ordinary state of mind not to enter a religion that goes against normal common sense.

For people who become anxious about such matters, it is of first importance to build up courage in face of their own destinies. For this, their first step would be to select a teacher who can inspire them with true courage.

Courage, along with love, is the quality most needed for the advancement of humanity.

Question 16
What are the Causes of Diseases
that are beyond Medical Knowledge?

Q: What are the real causes of diseases, such as mental illnesses and other disorders, that are almost untreatable through contemporary medical science?

A: For the most part, these disorders occur through the functioning of possessed thought. In other words, you could say that they are brought on by what are usually called 'possessing spirits'.

When a person's physical body functions in perfect order (free from illness or distorted behavior), it indicates that the life-light from the divine world is being projected to the physical world without any interference along the way. What are commonly called disease, misfortune, and abnormal behavior are manifested in the following process: first, the light coming from the divine world is stained in the subconscious world by the accumulation of the person's unharmonious thoughts (unharmonious karma); next, the stained waves are formed into various kinds of physical diseases, misfortunes or distorted behavior, determined by the shapes, or appearances, of the unharmonious thoughts; then those shapes manifest themselves.

However, in the case of the disorders indicated in the question, thought waves from other souls, rather than the person's own thoughts, are blocking the divine light. Among the person's ancestors, or spirits who have some connection with the person, there are some who still live in a confused world where lost souls exist. Delusional thought waves sent by those related, lost souls, are intercepting the light from the divine world, restricting the freedom of the person's physical body. If we say that a person can live perfectly with 100 candle power of life-light, then it is only natural for the physical body to be restricted when the flow of light waves has less than ten candle power.

In view of this, there are only two means of curing the illness: to either purify or deflect the stained thought waves that are intercepting the divine light from the sides. If science takes this approach, it can cure them. However, it seems as though present-day medicine has not yet advanced to that level. Because of this, people with spiritual faith have taken the method or radiating a powerful light wave to the lost souls through prayer, awakening them from their illusions.

In the case of mental disorders, some doctors conduct

electrical treatments on their patients, apparently trying to adjust the cerebral nerves through the shock produced. This is what I call the correction of mental wavelengths. However, since there are various kinds of obstructing thought waves (coming from lost souls), if electrical treatments of similar wavelengths are performed on all patients it will bring little effect.

Before considering this kind of treatment, it is important for people to know that mental disorders are, to begin with, triggered by the person's own mental state, which is responded to and affected by thought waves with a similar vibration coming from lost souls in the subconscious world. Then, once the cause is recognized, one has to begin by easing and disentangling the suppressed thoughts of the afflicted person.

As long as people think that all diseases arise from physical causes or from mental phenomena that stem from physical phenomena, the number of afflicted people will not decrease on the whole.

If, instead of limiting themselves to conventional methods, people in the medical fields would conduct their research from the viewpoint that diseases may also be caused by disharmony in a world external to the physical body, we will see the completion of three medical sciences: physical, mental, and spiritual. When this comes about, I think we may expect that the questionable, superstitious treatments being practiced here and there may gradually be curbed. I feel that as long as nations say that it is up to doctors to treat disease, they have an obligation to recommend this level of research to the medical world.

Question 17
Is it Effective to Change your Name or Avoid a Certain Direction?

Q: Is it possible to change one's destiny by changing one's name? Also, is it possible to find happiness by avoiding a certain direction, through aspect divination (making predictions through the study of directions)?

A: One's destiny does not improve just because one has changed one's name.

A person's surname represents the history (karma) of the ancestors, and the given name represents the karma from the person's previous lifetimes. So, by looking at both names it is possible to guess at a person's character and past destiny. However, the vibration of the name alone does not form the person's fate.

Before a person has a surname and a given name—in other words, before the person is born—there is already an underlying cause that will project the person's destiny in the coming lifetime. This underlying cause manifests itself when a person is born to a family having a certain surname, and is called by a certain given name. The name does not form the person's destiny, but it represents the person's karma from previous lifetimes. In other words, it shows what the person did and what kinds of thoughts he or she had during a past way of life.

Thus it is possible to make guesses about a person's destiny in this lifetime based on his or her habits and tendencies from previous lifetimes, through the study of names. But it is only a guess, and we are not to infer that the guesser can see a fate that has been firmly fixed.

Because fortune-tellers do not see something that is definite, they sometimes guess correctly, but in many cases they do not. In predictions based on names, the names have to be studied along with the dates of birth. Therefore, it is very wrong to tell a person's destiny only through the name without asking the date of birth. Even if experts in the field tell a person's destiny with additional reference to the date of birth, they are still just making inferences from the manifestation of the person's karma accumulated in previous lifetimes. So, although one might change one's name, which manifests one's karma from past lifetimes, this alone will not enable one to improve one's destiny. For that, one would have to correct the disharmonious karma itself—which means to correct the mistaken aspects of one's character and way of living.

What dissatisfies me most in fortune-telling by name is that most of the fortune-tellers start by attacking the flawed parts of a person's anticipated destiny.

Many of these fortune-tellers unequivocally state that if you keep your present name, you will definitely suffer from a serious illness at around which month of which year, or that you are ill-fated for marriage, or that your life will be short. This is the same as saying that your karma is such and so, and that unless you change your name, your unharmonious karma will be sure to manifest itself, as is, in your life. This kind of guidance will cause people to become strongly conscious of their unharmonious karma, and that will chain their destiny to their cause and effect from past lifetimes.

Since this approach implants a kind of obsessive preoccupation with past causes, it is far removed from the way to true spiritual freedom. Moreover, unless the fortune-teller is exceptionally great, it is difficult to discern a person's past cause and effect from the vibrations of the name, and then to foresee the person's true future. It is therefore advisable to limit the use of fortune-telling by name only to the occasions of naming a newborn baby.

Without changing one's name, one's destiny will change when one has thoroughly recognized one's strong and weak points, and has devoted oneself wholeheartedly to developing the strong points. The prospects are even brighter for people who have achieved true spiritual faith, since they have surpassed the realm of fortune-telling by name.

As it is written in Japanese, my name, Masahisa Goi, has a total stroke number of 19 or 20 (Kumazaki style), which is called an empty number, and indicates a very bad destiny from the viewpoint of any kind of fortune-telling by name. In addition, the primary destiny number, arrived at by combining the four strokes that form the 'i' of Goi with the eight strokes that form the 'Masa' of Masahisa, is twelve strokes, and this is also considered bad. Moreover, the arrangement of plus and minus (yin and yang) in my name is also considered unlucky. The only good point is the name Masahisa.

According to predictions, the overall idea was that I would be abundantly blessed until early adulthood, but in the latter half of my life, whatever I did would fall through in midstream, and misfortunes would continue one after another. In addition to this, I would have little to do with my parents and siblings, and would always be lonely. However, my destiny has turned out entirely the opposite of those predictions. Until early adulthood, my circumstances were not considered fortunate by ordinary standards, yet, I am glad to say, my parents are still in good health and my five brothers and sisters are well. Moreover, my destiny has risen abruptly from early adulthood up to the present. Quite the contrary of loneliness, I have a cheery and lively daily life.

It must either be that fortune-telling by name is incorrect, or that I was able to rise above the karmic boundaries of fortune-telling by name. If the latter is the case, it means that even if your name is unlucky, your destiny can change if you have changed spiritually.

In any case, the point I would like to make here is that human beings should let themselves be guided by teachings or organizations that help them jump into a bright and hopeful life, and should stay away from teachings or suggestions that cast dark shadows on their life.

I'd like to urge you to entrust your destiny entirely to God, who exists within you. It is certain that when you do your very best, God will open up your destiny. It is not good to peep at your destiny trembling with fear. The courage that it takes to bravely accept your own situation is the most powerful force for clearing your path ahead of you. Human beings, live with courage!

Next, let us turn to the subject of directions. Since the study of prediction by direction, or aspect divination, is based on extensive research, it is an authoritative, academically recognized system that cannot be denied. Therefore, if you believe that you can improve your destiny by avoiding a certain direction, according to the study of aspect divination, you may do so. However, what I feel concerned about is that in applying those studies and teachings, people might become timid or nervous about every little thing they do, which will bind their freedom.

I do not think it likely that people who have achieved great things went about their work by checking their every move with the study of aspect divination. When you strive forward, putting forth your best efforts, based on your belief in yourself, God (your Guardian Spirits and Divinity) naturally guides you to the direction that will best develop your destiny. If you feel that you cannot believe in yourself, what you can do is to think of your Guardian Spirits and Divinity again and again each day, asking them to protect and guide you in your actions. As you keep doing this, you will naturally come to believe in your destiny. Unless you make it a priority to instill in your mind the firm belief that God is always with you, over and above your belief in fortune-telling by name or the study of aspect divination, you will not be able to enter the road to your spiritual awakening.

Question 18
On Daily Mental Attitude

Q: What frame of mind do you think is most necessary for us in our daily life?

A: The first thing is to clearly recognize that a human being does not live alone, nor does the family live all by itself. Always be mindful of what kind of influence yours and your family's actions are having on society. It is important to keep this at the root of your thinking in daily life. When people think only about their family's happiness, it often makes them clash with their neighbors and become unsociable. This is why we need to make a habit of always wishing to be helpful to others, to avoid hurting others, and avoid hurting ourselves too. For everyone, the most important state of mind is the spirit of letting everyone and everything live to the fullest. The same is true for nations.

If everyone reaches this state of mind, it is certain that society will get better, the nation will get better, and the world will get better too, without any need for difficult theories. The way to let others come alive, and let ourselves come alive too, is love—only love.

Question 19
On what Jesus Christ said about Committing Adultery in your Heart

Q: Jesus Christ said something to the effect that a man who feels sexual desire when he looks at a woman has already committed adultery in his heart. If this is true, there is almost no man past adolescence who has not committed adultery. I would like to ask for your comments on this point.

A: When I was young, I was very much troubled by this. The idea that it is wrong even to think something in your mind is painful beyond expression. And the more pure-minded a young person is, the greater the pain becomes.

I do not treat the question of sexual desire with the

same strictness as did Jesus Christ. Strict words like those might be good medicine for some people, but they can cause enormous pain to conscientious people. If you only heard these words and knew no more about Him, you might tend to think that Jesus was not a very great person. However, when you think about the conditions of the time, you realize that there were so many lax and corrupt relations going on between men and women that if Jesus had not used such extreme words there would have been no effect at all. We have to consider the differences in the times when we think about those words.

I always explain that when mistaken thoughts come to mind, it is at the moment when the very same quantity of mistaken thoughts from the past is meant to vanish away. When sexual desire occurs, the harder you try to stop those thoughts, thinking that they are wrong, the more they will arise. So rather than trying to stop those thoughts from coming out, it will be easier to extinguish them when you focus your attention on other things.

Yet it can also be quite difficult to focus your attention on other things. Therefore, in this situation I say that it would be better to just leave the thoughts be. If you get upset about them, it will take more time to extinguish all the thoughts that keep popping up in your mind. When you have such thoughts, it means that what has been hidden at the bottom is now coming up to the surface; so when all those thoughts have surfaced, they will all have vanished, for certain. Men, in general, know through experience that those emerging thoughts are not so weak that they can be readily stopped when you try to stop them.

When the thought comes out, it does not mean that you have done something wrong. Sexual desire can even be considered an irresistible force to the male nature, and it is a force beyond the 'goodness' or 'badness' of physical human beings. If a man is blamed for the emergence of such thoughts at the sight of a woman, it will be unbearable. When this kind of thought comes up—in other words, at the time when the thought is about to vanish—your mental attitude and the way you deal with it will determine whether or not it forms an unharmonious cause in your future.

In any case, I suggest that you start by recognizing that all thoughts and all actions are manifestations of past karma, and that they start to vanish at the moment when they appear. At the same time, please refrain from thinking things that hurt you, so that you may align yourself more closely with the divine will. It would be best for human beings, particularly men, to live with dignity and confidence, without fretting or feeling timid. A person who is just cautious in his or her behavior, without a positive drive to do good, will not be able to do good work on a grand scale.

Question 20
How can you know all about a Person just by Hearing his or her Name?

Q: Goi Sensei[35], why is it that you can clearly perceive a person's character and behavior just by hearing his or her name? And how is it that you also know whether the person is alive or dead?

A: This is rather hard to explain, but let me try to give you an explanation that is easy to follow.

For me, the person's name does not matter. When an inquirer starts to convey a person's name to me, I instantly connect with that person's mind.

To explain it further, this world is made up entirely of light waves and thought waves. Each individual lives surrounded by his or her thought waves. For example, a person called Ms. 'A' lives in the midst of thought waves that she has been transmitting since past lifetimes. Ms. 'A' interacts with people and things that in some way relate to either the direct or indirect causes[36] of her own past thoughts. Each individual has his or her own particular world, and lives in that world while interacting with others to the extent that the parties have causative connections with each other.

The world of thought waves is called the 'subconscious world,' and when we are speaking of an individual it is called the 'subconscious body.' Each individual's thought waves and behavioral waves are depicted in his or her subconscious body. Those waves are instantly observed in my mind at the moment when the inquirer starts to convey that person's name to me. The reason why I can observe those waves is that, at that moment, I can empty my mind of all thoughts. My mind being empty, the character and destiny of Ms. 'A', depicted in her subconscious body, are projected into the emptiness.

This is because 'emptiness' is the same as expansion to the dimensions of the universe. Since Ms. 'A', who is a microcosm of the universe, lives in my mind expanded to the size of the universe, everything about her becomes clear to me. Even if the inquirer and Ms. 'A' have never met, the result is the same.

Why is the result the same? Let me explain the principle behind it. The fact that the inquirer and Ms. 'A' have never met refers only to the physical world. The fact that the inquirer is asking me about Ms. 'A' indicates that there is some sort of relationship between them from past lifetimes. If you have no connection with another person from past lifetimes, that person's name will never reach your lips. I can search for Ms. 'A' through this tiny indication.

When I have gotten to know about Ms. 'A', I do not tell the inquirer all that I have learned. I only convey what he or she truly needs to know.

In the case of marriage, I determine whether it is a good match or not after ascertaining the congeniality of the man's and the woman's characters and their karmic relationship from past lifetimes. Suppose a man and a woman who were hostile to each other in previous lifetimes are born in this world retaining intense grudges from the past. Even if, at the conscious level, they were in love and got married, once they were married, thoughts and feelings accumulated in their subconscious minds, carried over from past lifetimes, would start to appear on the surface, naturally rising to the conscious level through the karmic law of natural rotation. Then the couple would gradually start struggling with each other and it would lead to a big tragedy.

When couples with such karmic connections come to

consult with me on their intended marriage, no matter how they and the people around them might feel that they seem, on the surface, to be a good match, I flatly oppose the marriage. As a result, they sometimes bear a grudge against me, but this cannot be helped. When I am asked to mediate the conflicts between such people after marriage, it is not unusual for me to recommend their divorce unless they have an especially large number of children.

For couples in this situation, even if one tries to orient them toward respecting each other, in many cases the karmic connections are so deeply rooted that it would be utterly difficult for them to respect each other in this world. When religious leaders who do not know this principle try to force couples to respect each other, emphasizing the importance of harmony, the more time goes by the more difficult it becomes for the couple to sever their karmic interaction, and finally there could be killing or wounding. If it is firmly fixed that once a couple gets married they can never be parted, the opportunities for human deliverance will be narrowed because there are such cases.

True harmony exists when the right person is placed at the right location, and when the most suitable man is brought together with the most suitable woman. I hope that, in the future, there will be more and more people who can truly sense these matters and give good guidance to others.

I believe that people who always thank their Guardian Divinities and Spirits and ask for their protection will certainly be provided with a good spouse. In any case, it is best to always emanate bright thoughts.

At the moment when I hear the name of a good person with great depth of love, a very deep, loving spirit is projected to me, giving me a really pleasant feeling. When I hear the name of a wonderful artist, I get a truly wonderful feeling, too. The other day, when I saw a picture in the newspaper of Joseph Szigeti, the violinist, in his younger days, I got an exquisitely pleasant feeling. Superb music could be heard, or perceived, from the picture.

The spirit of love and good art have equal beauty. What I always see is a person's thoughts and feelings, not the physical body. This is because my true residence is not in this world of the physical body.

Next, the way I can tell whether a person is living or dead is from whether or not light waves from the individual spirit are flowing to the physical world.

In cases where the spiritual light waves have already stopped flowing to the physical world, but the subconscious body does not leave the physical body and the light waves to be sent to the physical body remain in the sub-conscious body like a storage battery, the person is still living in the physical world, although death is close. Once the stored light waves (life) have disappeared, the physical body will collapse at that time.

When we describe the relationship between the spiritual and subconscious worlds and the physical one, television offers us a really good analogy.

Suppose that, at a TV broadcasting station, a variety of dramas are being performed live. However, until you turn on the TV, and the programs are projected on the screen, you cannot see any of it. Once the TV is turned on and the electrical currents (light and sound waves) begin to flow, the images and sounds emitting from the broadcasting station will be transmitted through those waves, and appear on the TV screen, showing you a variety of scenes and activities.

The human physical body corresponds precisely to the television screen, and the spiritual world corresponds to the broadcasting station. The space between the broadcasting station and the TV set corresponds to the subconscious world. This is where the karmic causes and conditions that are to manifest themselves in the physical world move to and fro. Seen from the physical side (the perspective of the TV viewers), if there is no physical body (no TV screen), nothing seems to exist at all. There seems to be no human being, which indicates, in other words, 'death.' However, just as, at the broadcasting station, the dramas are still going on, in the spiritual and subconscious worlds the vibrations of life are still resonating. Human beings are still carrying on their activities. It is just that those activities are not projected on the TV screen.

I am at a standpoint where I can see the activities of human beings from all three perspectives: the spiritual world (the stage of the broadcasting station), the subconscious world, which is in the middle, and also the physical body (the TV screen).

Question 21
When Psychics Tell us about Criminals or Lost Articles

Q: There are psychics who, when asked about a theft or a lost article, reply that they were stolen by a person of approximately what age, facial features, and so on. Is this truly accurate?

A: Before saying whether it is accurate or not, my feeling would be that it is not the divine will to point out offenders or criminals through this kind of psychic perception.

Psychic perception is meant to come from God. If the guidance does not come directly from divine beings or high spirits, it might come from the lower spiritual world. Regardless of where it comes from, the guidance that one conveys should always be useful for the spiritual development of the disciples or the listeners.

Helping to make people out to be criminals by simply pointing out offenders—which means judging people on behalf of a particular person or a particular household—is not within the original mission of a person with psychic perception. A person with psychic perception should essentially be a person of true spiritual faith. Therefore, if psychics make guesses, or even assist people in hurting others, it means that they have wholly distanced themselves from the divine will. I would like you to appreciate the meaning of this before I go on to answer your question.

When a psychic replies that the offender is a person of about what age and with what sort of facial features, it is sometimes correct. On the other hand, there are also numerous cases where psychics look into the inquirer's subconscious, and name or indicate a person whom the inquirer suspects. The problem here is that psychics often believe that their answer is a message from God, since they, themselves, do not realize that they are naming an offender according to the suspicion of the inquirer.

Psychics who point out offenders in answer to such inquiries are functioning at a low spiritual level. They cannot distinguish divine messages from the thoughts of spirits residing in the subconscious world, and they believe that the words uttered through their own mouths are all divine messages. This is why it is not advisable to ask such psychics about a theft or similar matter. Rather, it would be best to pray to God (your Guardian Spirits and Divinity) while sitting quietly by yourself, reflecting upon your past attitude and asking pardon for any mistakes you may have made. Then, if having the lost or stolen article back would be good for you, it will be returned; and if having it back would not good for you, the article will not reappear.

It is a much greater loss to unsettle one's mind by letting one's thoughts run about in confusion than it is to lose things. The things that you need will surely come back to you. When I am asked about such matters, I first pray silently for the person, then I just tell the person clearly that an article that is to be returned will reappear, and that an article that is not to be returned will not reappear. I make it a rule not to touch upon the offender with even one word.

Even if you do not know the karmic explanation for why an article was stolen from you, there must be some karma involved. When you apologize to God for causing trouble to others and pray for the karma to be extinguished, generally speaking the missing article will come back. It is necessary for human beings to always aim at turning a misfortune into a blessing, and to discipline themselves into thinking that way.

Question 22
Do Mediums Truly Let us Hear the Voices of Deceased People from Other Worlds?

Q: *Does it ever happen that the spirit of a departed parent, brother, sister, or acquaintance comes to a medium and makes gestures or speaks through that person?*

A: Of course it does. But there are times when the spirit does not come, perhaps because of the level of the medium, or because of the circumstances at that time, or because the spirit being called has no interest in the physical world, or for whatever other reason.

Even when a spirit seems to have visited, it sometimes turns out to be a make-believe visit. This is done by a controlling spirit behind the medium, to avoid embarrassment to the medium. This controlling spirit looks into the subconscious mind of the client and, through the medium, imitates the past mannerisms of the departed person which have been recorded in the memory of the client.

Whether it is real or make-believe, I think it is a good learning experience for a person to see a seance once or twice. I say this because at the present time, when people are excessively caught up in mistaken beliefs about the physical body, there is something to be gained from knowing that there are other worlds besides the physical one, where souls continue to live after 'death.' This knowledge would surely give people an incentive to live their physical life more seriously, and it might awaken them to the need to purify their mind.

In this sense, I think that psychic research is a meaningful pursuit. In this area, though, caution is of the essence. Once you know about psychic perceptions, it is crucial not to be forever obsessed by the subject. After meeting a psychic person, you must absolutely never desire to possess the same kind of psychic abilities yourself. Never forget that what heightens you and saves you is always love, sincerity, and the courage to put love into practice. Everything else is merely training for fostering these qualities.

As people progress along the path of love and sincerity, even if they meet with hardships and it seems as though they are on the wrong path, God will never abandon them. For people to live truly and rightly, the most important thing is to firmly and positively believe that the day will most certainly come when their path will open up for them.

PRAYER FOR WORLD PEACE

At this point in time, are people on Earth happy or unhappy? If asked this question, most might reply that the world is presently in an unhappy state.

Why are people on Earth unhappy? It is because their thoughts are filled with animosity and conflict and their world abounds with imperfect, unharmonious conditions.

The world we live in has become quite small. The political measures and policies taken by the large, powerful nations immediately produce effects on the smaller ones; likewise, the events taking place in smaller countries have direct repercussions in the larger ones.

Today the life led by an individual cannot possibly be confined to that individual alone. Each person is inevitably influenced by the circumstances and attitudes in their country and the world. Consequently, I think we can say that there is no such thing as an individual life today. Individuals cannot help but respond to the conditions that prevail throughout the nation and humanity. Furthermore, no matter how capable a person is, or how much he or she has accomplished individually, that alone cannot cause the whole country or the human race to find happiness. Until nations and humanity as a whole free themselves from antagonistic emotions, and rise above their imperfect, unharmonious living conditions, there can be no true happiness for individuals.

Nowadays, wherever we look, the international conditions hold an ominous atmosphere that forebodes of a big war. If war has not yet broken out it is simply because that volatile atmosphere has not yet been ignited.

One never knows when war might break out or when natural disasters might occur. Surrounded by this kind of uncertainty, it is extremely difficult for individuals to live with a firm sense of happiness. In reflecting on this, it occurred to me that if there is no way for individual happiness to come about unless it is linked to the happiness of humanity, it will be important for us to change our perspective. We ought to try thinking of the individual and humanity as being one single entity, and conduct all our actions from that standpoint. This was the idea that gave birth to the prayer for world peace that I have been recommending to people.

World peace comes about when each individual lives in a peaceful setting. Likewise, when each individual lives in a peaceful setting, it means that world peace has been realized. Yet the present situation is quite the reverse.

True peace has not yet come forth either in the minds of individuals or throughout humanity. I think this becomes immediately clear when we take a close look either at the world conditions or into our own hearts.

Individuals, and the world as a whole, are always restless and uneasy. The short-lived happiness that most individuals experience today is only a fleeting moment amidst conditions that fluctuate from one instant to the next. It is not the steady kind of happiness that flows from the infinite source of our life. True happiness is something that we have to foster and develop from now on by cooperating with one another. If people keep clinging to a false sense of happiness that is not rooted in the infiniteness of life, there will be no way for true peace to emerge in this world.

The principal cause of this world's unhappiness occurred when we human beings forgot that we are all brothers and sisters whose lives flow from the one, great, all-inclusive life known as God. That was when we began to regard ourselves and others as separate entities, and embarked upon a lifestyle that disrupts the oneness of life and departs from the spirit of humanitarian love.

That sort of lifestyle has now become a habit. The notion that we and others are separate existences has generated a mass of unharmonious thought waves. Those waves have enveloped the whole of humanity and given rise to a variety of egocentric desires and emotions. These are what cause people to think that any person or country which infringes on their own individual interests—or on the interests of their country—is an enemy. As a result, even though there may be a handful of great people in today's society who try to conduct politics in keeping with principles of truth, the force of humanity's unharmonious thought waves is so violent that it prevents those people from putting those true principles into practice.

The world has become so populous that the actions of a few people are, in themselves, not sufficient to make the world change direction. For that, the power of a large mass of people is needed. There has to be a simple way for the power of the general population to be activated for the realization of world peace. Although there is no human being who, deep down, does not wish to have world peace, in our confused world the general public has no idea how to bring world peace into reality.

What the world absolutely needs now is a simple method for world peace that anyone can practice without strain or hardship. We need a method that will naturally bring people's hearts together without strenuous effort—a method that does not distinguish between our interests and the interests of others, but spontaneously fosters an awareness of our oneness with others. To develop this sense of oneness, each person must be able to release their preoccupation with gains and losses. This is the role of the prayer for world peace.

Here I would like to acquaint you with my view on the fundamental nature and way of living of human beings:

In his or her true state, a human being is not karmic or sinful. Human beings are lives that branch out from the one, great, divine life known as God. Each human being is continually protected by a Guardian Divinity and by Guardian Spirits who are the person's own awakened spiritual foremothers and forefathers.

All the sufferings of this world occur when human beings' mistaken thoughts, conceived during past lifetimes as well as the present one, take shape in this world in the process of fading away.

Any affliction, once it appears, is destined to vanish into nothingness. When suffering occurs, it is very important to firmly believe that this is fading away, and to think that from now on things will definitely get better. No matter how difficult the circumstances, forgive yourself and forgive others, love yourself and love others. If you live in this way, constantly speaking and acting in the spirit of love, sincerity, and forgiveness, always thanking your Guardian Spirits and Divinity for their protection, and praying for the peace of the world, you as an individual—and humanity as a whole—will be able to reach true spiritual freedom. This is what I think and put into practice.

May Peace Prevail on Earth.
May Peace be in our homes and countries.
May our missions be accomplished.
We thank you, Guardian Spirits
and Guardian Divinities.

If you continually hold these simple words in your heart, and let all your thoughts merge into them, a brighter way of life will naturally open up for you. Before you know it, your selfish or cliquish feelings will diminish and you will find yourself wishing for the happiness of all people. As this feeling of humanitarian love wells up within you, your individual character will gradually find wholeness and your lifestyle will strike a harmonious note. This, in itself, is the greatest thing that an individual can do for world peace.

I believe that prayer for world peace is the single most needed good action in today's world. It serves the dual aim of bringing peace to the individual life while at the same time playing a large role in the achievement of global peace.

NOTES

1. *Kuu* is sometimes translated as 'stillness,' 'emptiness' or 'nothingness.' Masahisa Goi explains: *Kuu is not a nihilistic or negative condition. It contains nothing, yet everything. It is the infiniteness of life itself—divinity itself—living vibrantly.*

2. Here, 'karmic' refers to disharmonious vibrations that had accumulated in the world through cycles of cause and effect. Refer to Chapters 3-5.

3. *Sakyamuni* refers to the saint whose teachings formed the basis of Buddhism. The spelling 'Shakamuni,' is also commonly used. *Gautama* and *Shakuson* also refer to *Sakyamuni.*

4. The term used is *Chokurei. Choku* means 'direct' and *rei* means 'spirit'. *Chokurei* is the light emanating directly from God to form the origin of humanity. *Chokurei* could be translated as 'God in the human world', 'Direct Spirit', or 'Divine Self.' (Refer to Figures 1 and 2 in Chapter 3.)

5. The term used is *Bunrei*. *Bun* means 'divide' or 'division,' and '*rei* means 'spirit.' *Bunrei* means 'divided spirit', 'division of God,' or 'spirit emanating from the Direct Spirit of God.'

6. Essentially, The word *karma* means 'work.' It is the work, or creative activity, of a person's thought waves.

In these chapters, the terms 'karma' or 'karmic' refer to the activity of thought waves that were emitted after human beings forgot their original identity as divine beings. Or, they may refer to disharmonious vibrations that have accumulated in the subconscious body and sub-conscious world through cycles of karmic cause and effect.

7. The term used is *Inyô*. *In* refers to minus energy, and *yô* refers to plus energy.

8. The term used is *Shugojin*. *Shugo* means guidance and protection. *Jin* means God, Divinity, or Deity. *Shugojin* may also be translated as 'Guardian Angel.'

9. *Konpaku*: *Kon* refers to thoughts that have accumulated in the subconscious body, while *paku* refers to material elements. When we call a spirit *konpaku* we are referring to the physical human being.

10. This refers to the Direct Spirit of God. See Note 4.

11. The quoted phrases are not taken from Bible. The author, himself, attributes them to Jesus.

12. The term used is *Shûchaku*, sometimes translated as 'attachment.' *Shûchaku* does not refer to harmonious attachments such as faithfulness and devotion, but rather to obstructive attachments such as fixed ideas or obsessiveness.

13. Sanskrit. A Bodhisattva is one who is born into this world having made a vow to work for the deliverance of others. In Japanese, Bodhisattva is called *Bosatsu*.

14. Kobo Daishi means 'The Great Teacher Kobo.' He lived from 774 to 835 A.D., known as the priest Kukai. Kobo Daishi founded the Shingon sect of Buddhism in Japan after returning from China, where he was entrusted with sacred teachings and practices called *Mikkyô*.

15. In the original, the term used is *ningen*, which means 'human being(s).' The word has no masculine or feminine gender.

GOD AND MAN

16. A 'physical human being' is someone who lives without an awareness of his or her divinity.

17. The phrase in Japanese is *Shiki soku Zekkuu, Kuu soku zesshiki*, a phrase frequently used in Buddhism.

18. Refer to Figures 2 and 3 in Chapters 3 and 4.

19. In this translation the terms 'destiny' and 'fate' are used interchangeably. In Japanese the word is *unmei*. *Un* means 'move' or 'carry' and *mei* means 'life'. Thus *unmei* ('destiny' or 'fate') is the sequence of conditions or events that 'carry' our life.

20. 'Phenomenal' refers to the visible or tangible conditions in the physical (material) world.

21. The world of 'shapes and forms' is the same as the physical, or phenomenal world.

22. The name of the poet is Genzo Sarashina.

23. *Ten to Chi wo Tsunagu Mono* means 'One who Connects Heaven with Earth.' The book can be obtained in Japanese

from Byakko Press. See www.ByakkoPress.ne.jp for news of upcoming translations.

24. An *In* is a means of attracting and emitting harmonizing energy by keeping one's breathing peaceful while making precise movements with the hands, arms, and fingers.

25. The term used here is *Reikon*. *Rei* refers to the spirit, while *kon* refers to thoughts that have accumulated in the subconscious body. When we say *reikon* we are referring to the spirit accompanied by its accumulated thought waves. *Reikon* is translated as either 'spirit' or 'soul.'

26. The expression used is *Chokurei sono mono*. Refer to Note 4.

27. *Kon* refers to subconscious elements: thoughts that have accumulated in the subconscious body. (Refer to Fig. 3 in Chapter 4.)

28. *Haku*, or *paku*, refers to material elements. (Refer to Figure 3 in Chapter 4.)

29. The God or Goddess of Mercy (called *Avalokites-vara* in Sanskrit) is a manifestation of the merciful aspect of

God's love.

30. Plus and minus functions can also be referred to as 'Ying and Yang.'

31. Here, 'physical human beings' refers to people who are easily misled because they are unaware of their true identity as infinite (divine) beings.

32. The *Kegon* Sutra is called the *Avatamska* Sutra in Sanskrit.

33. A mandala is a round graph, or picture, that represents the truth of the universe and the structure of heaven and earth.

34. See Note 25.

35. *Goi Sensei* refers to the author, Masahisa Goi. The term *Sensei* means 'teacher' or 'advanced person.'

36. In this translation, indirect causes have also been called 'triggers.'

A MESSAGE TO OUR READERS

In 1955, two years after writing this book, Masahisa Goi initiated a worldwide movement of prayer for world peace, based on the peace prayer and message *May Peace Prevail on Earth*.

Several organizations have formed themselves around Mr. Goi's vision for peace, including the Byakko Shinko Kai, the World Peace Prayer Society, and the Goi Peace Foundation. Interested people may contact these organizations for further information. The addresses are shown below:

Byakko Shinko Kai

a worldwide grassroots peace initiative aimed at assisting all people in furthering their highest spiritual aspirations and goals.
812-1 Hitoana, Fujinomiya, Shizuoka 418-0102 Japan
Phone [+81] (0) 544-29-5100 Fax [+81] (0) 544-29-5111
E-mail: gbs1357@quartz.ocn.ne.jp
http://www.byakko.or.jp

The World Peace Prayer Society

a Non-Governmental Organization (NGO) associated with
the Dept. of Public Information at the United Nations;
dedicated to spreading the non-sectarian message and prayer
May Peace Prevail on Earth
26 Benton Road, Wassaic, NY 12592 USA
E-mail: peacepal@worldpeace.org
http://www.worldpeace.org

The Goi Peace Foundation

working to build a global peace network uniting our hearts
and our wisdom for world peace;
established in Tokyo with the approval of
the Japanese Ministry of Education
Heiwa Daiichi Bldg. 1-4-5 Hirakawa-cho
Chiyoda-ku, Tokyo 102-0093 Japan
Phone [+81] (0) 33265-2071 Fax [+81] (0) 33239-0919
E-mail: info@goipeace.or.jp
http://www.goipeace.or.jp